Tostig Godwinson, Earl of Northumbria

Tostig Godwinson, Earl of Northumbria

Tristram Cole

Also by the author:

The Annelid Poet
the fawn and the leaf

Tostig Godwinson, Earl of Northumbria
Copyright © 2016 by Tristram Cole
All rights reserved. Except for brief passages quoted in a newspaper, online, or in some other forum of the media, no part of this publication may be reproduced or transmitted in any form or by any means other than vellum without express written permission of the author.

First edition, printed by CreateSpace

ISBN-13: 978-1482351439
ISBN-10: 1482351439

To my brother Nick

TOSTIG GODWINSON, EARL OF NORTHUMBRIA

The Persons of the Play

England
EDWARD "the Confessor," King of England
HAROLD Godwinson, Earl of Wessex
TOSTIG Godwinson, Earl of Northumbria and Harold's brother
EDITH Swannhals, Harold's Dane-wife
EDWIN, Earl of Mercia
MORCAR, Edwin's brother
ROBERT Fitz-Wimark, Edward's friend
AELDRED, Archbishop of York
STIGAND, Archbishop of Canterbury
KENRICK, Thegn of Easingwold

France
WILLIAM, Duke of Normandy
William FITZ-OSBERN, the duke's steward
Bishop ODO of Bayeux
ROB & WILL, the duke's two sons
Abbot LANFRANC

Norway
Harald Sigurdsson aka HARDRADA, King of Norway
EYSTEIN Orre, Chief Norse nobleman
LEIF Andreasson, Norse nobleman
ARNULF Ulson, Norse nobleman
GUNNAR Streelkin, Norse nobleman
THIODULF, a skald
FRIREK, Norse warrior

Other players

A THEGN of Mercia	FREYA, servant of Harold
COUNT Guy of Ponthieu	QUEEN Edith, Edward's wife
Two HIRELINGS, Tostig's men	ELSA, servant of Eystein
An EALDORMAN	HEARTH BOY

Various nobles, clerks, soldiers, servants, housecarls, etc.

The Scene
Northern Europe, the eleventh century

Tostig Godwinson, Earl of Northumbria

Act I scene 1: London. The king's great hall on Thorney Island.

EDWARD sits on a large throne. AELDRED stands nearby. A clerk and HEARTH BOY are also present. Housecarls stand guard.

AELDRED   Clerk, get the hearth boy there.
    Clerk summons HEARTH BOY
HEARTH BOY   Yes, your majesty?
EDWARD   It is very cold in the hall.
HEARTH BOY   Is it, your majesty?
EDWARD   It is not so very cold out of doors.
HEARTH BOY   No, your majesty.
EDWARD   Summer. Much is done. *(Pause)* Fetch the mantle from my wardrobe.
HEARTH BOY   But the doors are locked, your majesty, and I have no key.
AELDRED   Clerk, obtain the key of the chamberlain.

EDWARD Go now. The casements too – those along the way –
shut them – not all though – just some. *(Exeunt clerk and
HEARTH BOY. The clerk returns shortly after.)* So much left.
   Pause
AELDRED Your highness, allow me to explain this in
   A different way: with the Hampstead quarries emptied
   Stone must be carted from further afield.
   More carts and oxen will be necessary
   If the work's to proceed with a like alacrity.
EDWARD It's God's will, Archbishop. If I had made that pil-
grimage. The queen says stone masons are rough men.
AELDRED My Lord, they are rough – but perhaps it takes
   Coarse men to make things delicate of mind,
   So that a balance obtain between them.
EDWARD It is a rough life here. God makes things hard for
righteous kings – other men too – not sinners.
AELDRED Yes, your majesty – sinners have the easier path.
EDWARD But only to damnation – after they die – though
before then –
   Enter KENRICK and EDWIN
AELDRED *(to EDWIN)* Mercia, why is this man here?!
KENRICK Your majesty, Northumbria is near revolt.
   No longer will the people shape dismay
   To fit a cruel martial law. And so
   Myself, and many more distinguished lords –
   At threat of violence from the shires – have come
   In forcèd embassy to see you,
   And urge your swift relief from the ruinous
   Depredations of our tyrant earl.
AELDRED *(to EDWARD)* The Thegn of Easingwold, my lord.
   (Aside to KENRICK) Kenrick, your manner is indecorous.
EDWARD Outside are they – awaiting my words?
KENRICK My liege, they wait most desp'rately
   Upon your calling, and swear by joint

Allegiance on no account to quit this place
Until they've shared just audience with you,
Their sovereign.
EDWARD *(to AELDRED)* Is Wessex gone, do you suppose?
AELDRED *(to EDWARD)* Shall I order him sent for? He cannot be long on the road now.
EDWARD What are those papers you have there?
KENRICK These, sire, are their doleful suits –
So many summarizèd losses though,
Reduced to blocked and charted ciphers,*
Must seem a mere recrimination of numbers,*
Or minutiae to a bookkeeper.
There is hard suffering in the north,
Your majesty, and not pages but only men
May tell it.
EDWARD *(taking the papers)* They are very angry – dispossessed and therefore angry. No, this is too much – bring them in. Bring in *(Consults papers)* the Thegn of Tinmouth – Tynemouth – and the abbot too. Oh, bring them all in! *(To AELDRED, handing him the papers)* Call forth whom you will – we shall hear him.
AELDRED Reeve of Durham, come forward and address your king.
  Enter REEVE
REEVE Most pious king – your excellency – Durham, seventh shire of Northumbria and richest by far, is despoiled in some 300 hide.* An ealdorman is dead and his sons are missing.
EDWARD 300 hide, Archbishop! 300 hide!
AELDRED Thegn of Harrowgate, enter and relate your woes.
  Enter HARROWGATE
HARROWGATE Harrowgate's secure, your highness, but the

---

cipher [1] something without weight, value, or influence [2] number
So many...of numbers i.e. the losses, presented in this format, appear trivial and therefore open to recrimination
hide unit of land area, here about 75 acres

people agitate, there being no shire courts to hear appeals, nor markets safe enough for surplus.
AELDRED   Thegn of Haxby – Haxby – come forward.
   Enter HAXBY
HAXBY   Mine humble, honest king – Haxby, of a quarter wapentake,* hath, since Godwinson's coming, beared it hard, with several beasts stole or killed – and men too, I wot.* E'en right afore Nones* some brigands set a hayrick burning, and thence a shed – without cause, majesty – so that two died there.
AELDRED   Who is the leader of this embassy?
EDWIN   The Thegn of Easingwold brought these men down
   Into Mercia, whence I set forth, attending,
   For fear lest my own earldom take infection
   From the growth and spread of this malignity.
   Reenter HEARTH BOY with mantle, which he gives to EDWARD
EDWARD   The hall should be cleared – boards bestowed. This suffering – indignities. How long, oh Lord? Yes. Prepare a royal table – somewhat apart – for our attendance *(Voices offstage)* – and the archbishop *(Voices become clamorous)* – and the Earl of Mercia –
   He rises to leave
AELDRED   What is that stirring?
EDWARD   Belike* some riot will ensue.
AELDRED   Housecarls!*
TOSTIG *(offstage)* Make way! You've poisoners enough within!
   He enters
   Hath your majesty not yet announced

---

wapentake   Danish term corresponding to the English "hundred," an area of farmland deemed capable of supporting one hundred armed men and supplying them, if called upon, to the local militia
wot   (archaic) know
Nones   the fifth or seventh day of the month on the Julian calendar, depending on the position of the Ides
belike   (archaic) most likely; probably
housecarl   member of the household troops of a king or nobleman, always heavily armed and usu. highly trained

The manner of my ordeal?* Shall it be scalding,
Haxby? Or some other rack and torture?
Easingwold, am I to be branded thief
For my nose and ears, or wilt thou clap me traitor –
Leave me dangling at the gibbet?
What manner of men are you th't can pass
O'er oaths and homage as customs of no worth
When a few bandits interpose themselves
'Twixt chaos and the peace? You could come
To me direct, in due fealty – try my honor –
And who can say you'd not leave well-pleased
With my solutions? Aye, who can,
'Cause you chose rather to accost your overlord
Like he were some ill-mannered smith i' the street
You'd pump for change!

KENRICK   I object to this rough treatment, sir.
EDWARD   Men can be rough, indeed.
TOSTIG   Your majesty,
I'm done abusing these faithless mendicants.
Moreover, I think I've devised a solution
'Twill well please both parties of offence –
That much I'm owed.
I offer you, my lord, in short,
An exchange most advantageous to the crown:
All the reputed vagabonds feasting
In Northumbria for the thankless privilege
Of strangling these sorry beggars.

REEVE   Where is the Ealdorman Aegilfe – why don't you speak of him or his kin?
KENRICK   Or the Thegn of Beningbrough, or Lord Gospatric, Or many more besides.
TOSTIG   You'll hear no false accounts from me:

---

ordeal   method of determining the guilt or innocence of an accused person by subjecting him/her to a dangerous and often painful physical test, the outcome of which was regarded as an indication of divine judgment

Many nobles who could not abide
My strict rule* have, as it were, fled
The monastery to see* elsewhere in the realm.
But their abandoned cells, my sovereign,
Have been duly filled, and by clerics* of
A higher order. Do you, too, Easingwold,
Choose to join those monks in cenobitic* exile?
KENRICK   I choose only to make certain our king
Has true reports of your dealings in Northumbria.
The men whom this sham earl claims as brigands
Comprise his own pestilent retainer –
Our land's chewed bare by the unfiefèd locusts
He doth put to it! Every day men die
By their rapacious swords.
TOSTIG   What sayest his majesty to all these outrages?
Surely some man ought to hang in this!
   EDWARD whispers to AELDRED
AELDRED   The king is much disturbed by these proceedings
And bids me force amends between you –
Or some brief peace at least – until such time
As the present health of Northumbria
May be gleaned from more unbiased report.
   EDWARD whispers again to AELDRED
He will retire now unto his private chambers,
To commune there with Our Holy Lord
And meditate on this conflict. The feast is off
And the hall torches will be extinguished.
EDWIN *(aside to AELDRED)* Your greatness knows full well just what
And who may be disputed here. Why does
The king choose such boorish favorites?

---

rule set of precepts observed by a monastic order
see a cathedral town; episcopal jurisdiction or authority
cleric member of the clergy
cenobitic of or relating to communal monasticism

AELDRED   Guard thy tongue, Mercia, if thou wouldst stay
    Within the pale of his affections – and mine.
       Exeunt EDWARD and AELDRED at one side, then others
       opposite. TOSTIG remains.
TOSTIG   Fools all! That I should play the jester!
    E'en so. There's too much scorn to pile on –
    Too much anger – too much disgust.
    Ah, the heart: unending foam and flow –
    So much seething – such commotion.
       Pause
    There was a time I understood –
    At a nonce* could tell which way to feel –
    A moment when between these several parts
    Prevailed a calm, one brief heart-stricken day
    Upon which I could not think or grieve but,
    As I walked the street – to keep breathing
    Merely – I encountered two men in a fight
    Over some obscurity, and for a fleeting
    Instant felt a keenness, life. 'Twas then,
    Without conscious reference to the fray,
    There murmured something inwardly th't seemed
    To say, "This is not part of thine," and so
    I turned and strode away from such as once
    Had crazed my meditations and sent me storming in
    To maul them.
    What was it wasn't "thine" or mine
    Th't soothed that single hour of my yearning,
    Made it seem more of myself than myself?
    What was it now since dragged away, howling,
    Over spikes and barbs? It is all too cruel
    And I am in a frenzy for it.
       Exit

At a nonce instantly; immediately

Act I scene 2: The coast of Ponthieu.

Enter HAROLD and COUNT

HAROLD   Well Count, you've sharper rocks than we do, that I'll grant ye.
COUNT   Perhaps you should consider importing them.
HAROLD   I can't get from Winchelsea to Flanders without wrecking, Count. You'd best keep them here.
COUNT   We have many lovely trees too.
HAROLD   Yes, I can see that you do – very straight and hearty.
COUNT   Can I interest you in a dilapidated bridge?
HAROLD   How 'bout a ship, Count? – A seaworthy vessel
To send and set my feet again on the shores
Of England.
COUNT   Do you mean to have them amputated?
HAROLD   *(after a moment)* I have not yet made up my mind.
Ah, here are horsemen – this must be William's posse.
COUNT   William has excellent surgeons.
HAROLD   Really Count, I –
Enter WILLIAM with noblemen and attendants
WILLIAM   Ponthieu, stop troubling this man with your strangeness. He is the son of Godwin, and Edward's most trusted earl.
COUNT   I do not choose to be strange, Duke.
WILLIAM   No, of course you don't. You may leave us Count. *(Exit COUNT)* Tedious old codger. So Godwinson, have you been exiled again? Where's the rest of your retinue?
HAROLD   Do you mean to take me as a prisoner
To Normandy or send me back to Albion?*
WILLIAM   I mean to keep you with me for a while,
But not as hostage.
HAROLD   Ah then: invitee.

Albion (archaic) poetic term for England or Britain

WILLIAM   I've expeditions underway in Brittany
   From which I cannot be detained.
HAROLD   Nor do
   I wish to keep you from them, worthy duke –
   I shall therefore ride with you to Rouen,
   And from thence seek transport across the channel.
WILLIAM   You will accompany me for a time.
HAROLD   To what purpose?
   WILLIAM knocks HAROLD down
WILLIAM   Best you keep from baiting me, Earl,
   If you treasure much your dignity.
HAROLD   What dignity's there can't plead for freedom?!
WILLIAM   Stay on the ground there, man! I will be king
   Of England. When Edward chucked out Godwin
   And his kin for murdering his Norman guests,
   I did journey there to make stern protest
   'Gainst your lives, and it was then that first
   Your Edward promised me the crown, since which
   Many times he hath remembered it to me –
   In his meekness made such tenderings
   As would've signified a forfeiture
   Of realm to more ignorant regard. Therefore
   Keep you in the dirt there and listen till
   I have done. Do not incense me further –
   It would go hard with the Witan council*
   If I returned you dead, and I do not know
   How they're disposed to my succession.
   King Edward did – despite my harsh remonstrance –
   Restore you to your wonted titles, take
   You back into his feeble fold, like so many
   Scraggly and bewildered ewes.

Witan council assembly of the Anglo-Saxon ruling elite, both lay and ecclesiastical, which met with the king from time to time and advised him on matters of national importance; the Witan also played a significant role in the selection and ratification of a king's successor

It cannot now be long until his crook drop
Wessex, so get you up – make you my liegeman.
HAROLD *(getting to his feet)* Will a mount be provided, Duke…or shall I be dragged?
WILLIAM *(to attendant)* Bring him his horse, sirrah.* *(To all)* We ride to Brittany.

Act I scene 3: England. The western forests.

A horn sounds in the distance. Enter EDWARD and ROBERT.

ROBERT   Your majesty – your grace – the horn is blown – the hounds are cast.
EDWARD   Oh Robert.
ROBERT   Your grace – are you unwell?
EDWARD   I am not.
ROBERT   Sit you down, sire. What is it causing you such distress?
EDWARD   Robert, there is much evil in the world.
ROBERT   On that we have accord.
EDWARD   In England too – most detrimentally.
ROBERT   It does seem so, my lord.
EDWARD   I prayed for you this tierce,* between the hunts.
ROBERT   For me, your grace?
EDWARD   One prayer for every tine on the morning stag.
ROBERT   Then I trust there were at least ten?*
EDWARD   Northumbria!
ROBERT   Your majesty –
EDWARD   Oh!
ROBERT   Your majesty, the revolt will be quelled – You need only give over the earl. I had

---

sirrah   (archaic) term of address for an inferior, often expressing contempt
tierce   third of the seven canonical hours, usu. three hours after sunrise
at least ten   until a stag had ten or more points on its antlers ("hart of ten") it was not considered worthy of hunting

Informed you as soon as the second hunt was done.
EDWARD   My eldest friend, Lord.
ROBERT   Messengers have been dispatched to bring
  Earl Harold back from Flanders.
EDWARD   My eldest.
ROBERT   I apologize, your majesty, but I knew
  You'd not yet want to hear it – that your penchant,
  On a day of chase, is for hoof beats
  And the horn, not officious news.
EDWARD   Northumbria has never lied to me.
ROBERT   Has he not?
EDWARD   He is rough – sometimes.
ROBERT   Tostig Godwinson, your grace, is a hart
  That can't be brought to bay.*
EDWARD   Is that possible?
ROBERT   It's a figure of speech, my lord.
EDWARD   What should I do, Robert?
ROBERT   I don't know, sire – perhaps he should be chased
  away.
EDWARD   Back into the covert?*
  Voices and barking offstage
ROBERT   Well – I suppose so. Though if you aren't sure you
  should consult your ministers.
  Voices and barking grow louder. Voice offstage: "Tally Ho!"
EDWARD   Yes. Robert, let us finish this hunt.
ROBERT   Gladly, your majesty. I'd have done
  With statecraft. The stag is startled out –
  Let's set him to roaring! *(Pause)* Sire?
EDWARD   *(after praying silently)* Amen. I hear hounds.
  Exeunt

---

brought to bay (hunting) forced to face its pursuers
covert (hunting) a wood or thicket affording cover for game

Act I scene 4: England. A roadway in Northumbria.

TOSTIG and two HIRELINGS are waiting in ambush

TOSTIG   Well, someone comes up the road.
HIRELING 1   It isn't him, my lord.
HIRELING 2   Couple o' lasses with buckets. *(To HIRELING 1)* Let's jump them instead.
  Enter two peasant girls, laden, who giggle as they cross the stage, exiting opposite
TOSTIG   *(aside)* What idiocy this waiting is. *(Aloud)* Enough – I won't hunker and skulk any longer. *(Aside)* Farewell, sir.
HIRELING 1   They are coming.
TOSTIG   Are you sure?
HIRELING 1   My lord, I am – it is the thegn and some two or three others well-armed.
TOSTIG   Wait till they go by.
  Enter KENRICK and several ATTENDANTS
KENRICK   What most surprised me was the ease of its passage –
  Like the man had been canonized, not usurped.
ATTENDANT 1   Where we stood outside the crowd was most subdued.
ATTENDANT 2   Likely they had some foreknowledge.
KENRICK   It is, and also like they realized,
  Without King Edward's fixed imprimatur,
  The resolution won't be binding.
ATTENDANT 2   We shall get it, sire.
KENRICK   If to do so meant another, less humble
  March toward London, I would gladly join the ranks
  Of young Morcar's most unguarded flank.
  In truth, I'd risk my hearth and family
  For –
TOSTIG   *(revealing himself)* Come you from the York assembly?
ATTENDANT 2   You address a thegn, sirrah!

TOSTIG   Indeed, or one that was, as I was earl.
> *HIRELINGS take KENRICK and ATTENDANTS by surprise and disarm them*

(*To HIRELINGS*) Take them to that barn – (*To ATTENDANTS*) and keep quiet lest your lord be silenced. (*Exeunt HIRELINGS leading ATTENDANTS. To KENRICK.*) Was it you brought all this about, pilfered my treasury, murdered the men and women of my palace? Put a boy up to replace me?! If you'll lead men, Kenrick, if you'll give out just what's to be done and not one writ more, they'll still betray you – they'll still not think you just or grateful. Either you're an oaf or an assassin for them to topple their unwavering devotion on…and crush to pulp. If you'll lead men, Kenrick – truly lead them – then they'll despise you – prick you to false purposes and treacherously misguide you.

KENRICK   Do your spurs bleed – does your sword drip gore – because of me – of what I've done? You are misguided, misled, but is it out of my discountenancing?

TOSTIG   Yours is the head and top of it I should lop off.

KENRICK   And what have I done in bringing my men up the road here, in attending a most needful assembly, in challenging your lies before the king, in praying that – for wife and child – my life not end in this place? Say what it is?

TOSTIG   I am not here to kill you. That is not why I'm here.

KENRICK   Then let me go.

TOSTIG   I cannot do that either.

KENRICK   So this is purgatory then, the road from York to Easingwold. We can't stay here forever, Godwinson. I have my surety.* Which way wilt thou go?
> *Pause*

TOSTIG   What happened on my estate in York?

KENRICK   I do not know. The manor was left unprotected.

---

surety [1] formal pledge or legal instrument granting security against loss, damage, or default [2] (obsolete) means of assurance or safety, in this case religious

I was not present. *(TOSTIG wounds KENRICK)* Oh Jesus! Oh my loving –
  TOSTIG kills KENRICK. Pause.
TOSTIG   Can a man be made thus for destruction? What hand is here? What eye? What brains for believing?
  Pause
  Damn ye, Kenrick.
  Reenter HIRELING 1
HIRELING 1   You said –
TOSTIG   Aye, what did I say?: "Hold and do not harm." Didst thou?
HIRELING 1   My lord, they struggled against us when the thegn cried out – we had to beat them down. I fear one or two may have died.
TOSTIG   Leave them tied up in the byre.*
HIRELING 1   *(looking at the body)* What about him?

Act I scene 5: Brittany. A large tent within the Norman encampment.

WILLIAM is dictating to a clerk. Servants enter and exit throughout, setting a table around which benches have been arranged, except at one end where there are two chairs and a bible. The table has already been provided with cups and a jug of ale. It is raining.

WILLIAM   And no more about honeybees. Give me instead, rather, another account of servants fornicating in the scullery. If you want honey then you put up with bees. *(Enter FITZ-OSBERN with reliquary)* Very sorry to hear about your abscess. Have the…allodial* –

---

byre   cowshed; barn
allodial   describes land owned independently and thus not subject to any feudal dues

FITZ-OSBERN Quitrent.*
WILLIAM Yes, quitrent figures tabulated by district for my
   inspection. Yours, William. *(To clerk)* Leave us – that will
   be all. *(Exit clerk)* Just sending out the weekly sympathies.
FITZ-OSBERN So the duchess is well, I trust.
WILLIAM If lustily complaining be a sign of health.
FITZ-OSBERN Lanfranc did bid me bring this to you.
   He gives WILLIAM reliquary
WILLIAM   Why
   Is he not here himself as I had asked?
FITZ-OSBERN He refused to enter the camp, my lord,
   Though I did insist on your particular
   Request. He thought 'twould be discordant with
   The rule.
WILLIAM But snatching relics from the shrines
   Of churches is somehow in accord?! Just
   As well – he had but scant use here.
FITZ-OSBERN Whose artifacts are they, sire?
WILLIAM   I don't know –
   Somebody's veil or finger or bit of shoe –
   Read the inscription.
   He hands reliquary back to FITZ-OSBERN
FITZ-OSBERN *(reading)* Tudwal – femur
   Of Tudwal – doesn't say which one.
   He returns reliquary to WILLIAM
WILLIAM Rather a small casket for a femur.
   He sets reliquary on the table, drapes it with a tapis, and
   puts the bible on top*
   I will step out. Go – call our guests.
   Be sure that Harold finds his place of honor.
   They exit at opposite sides, then FITZ-OSBERN returns followed by several Norman NOBLES, who take seats at the

---

quitrent fixed rent paid by the tenant of a freehold (an estate held in fee for life) in lieu of other feudal obligations
tapis small tapestry or decorated cloth

benches around the table. The NOBLES, one of whom already seems intoxicated, help themselves to the ale.

NOBLE 1 *(to servant)* More ale here, tapster.

NOBLE 2   Less drizzle for me.

NOBLE 3 *(to servant)* Sirrah, what's on the boards tonight? I saw capons* out back and lots of fish racked up.

NOBLE 1   I smell roast onions.

NOBLE 2   I smell rain.

NOBLE 3   We sure gave those Bretonese a soaking.

ODO   Bretons, and there wasn't hardly a scrum formed.

NOBLE 2   The tent's leaking.

Reenter WILLIAM

WILLIAM   Greetings men. Well, after today's
Brief and bloody contest I'm afraid
That skirmishing and negotiation will
Not long support your appetites. It can't
Be helped – these Breton men daren't meet us
In the field again. Even so – *(aside to FITZ-OSBERN)* Where is he?

Exit FITZ-OSBERN

Yet still, having so fed upon your enemies –
Devoured them, as it were…

He trails off, distracted

NOBLE 1   Bring out the capons!

NOBLE 3   We chewed 'em up, my lord, but then we spat 'em out – therefore we're most hungry.

NOBLE 1 *(now quite drunk)* I hope no one swallowed any – that's excommunibacle.

WILLIAM   If you all will – just – silence now! – Ah, here he is. *(Reenter FITZ-OSBERN with HAROLD)* Welcome Harold. Come – sit here beside me. *(Aside to HAROLD)* What kept you?

HAROLD *(aloud)* Sorry to 've delayed the feasting. My horse

---

capon   rooster that has been castrated and fattened when young to improve the food quality of its flesh

was stuck in mud. I had walked through camp but I've only got one boot.
NOBLE 3   What happened to the other?
HAROLD   Wolves.
ODO   That's not true. The earl's boot was shorn away by an axe in the combat – the axeman's head then suffered like division by Harold's sword.
WILLIAM   The earl's conduct here in Brittany has but
Confirmed – in our more modest conflict –
The truth of his Welsh adversaries'
Awed accounts, who fought in Gruffydd's shield wall
And fled the field in rout. That is why
We honor him this night, and seek for his
Allegiance and support as Normandy
Surges, with the force of moment,
Ineluctably across the channel,
And why we ask that –
NOBLE 1   Drink to the Englishman!
WILLIAM   Remove this man, Fitz-Osbern.
NOBLE 1   *(singing)* For he's a jolly good –
WILLIAM   At once!
NOBLE 1   But he is, isn't he?
FITZ-OSBERN   That's really not the point. Up you go.
NOBLE 1   I don't understand.
WILLIAM   No you don't, fool!
   Exit FITZ-OSBERN with NOBLE 1. FITZ-OSBERN returns a short time after.
Lastly, I had asked, before this drunkard's
Witlessness, if you would take to wife
My daughter, Adeliza, that our joint pledge'd
Be further consecrated by the grafting
Of our family lines. Now, Earl Harold,
How make you in reply to all that I
Have said?

HAROLD   There is so much to reply to!
   First, I must thank you for those generous remarks
   Concerning my performance as commander,
   And commend you on such a brave and robust band
   Of hearth companions!
WILLIAM   Continue, good earl.
HAROLD   Never have I fought among men in whom
   Bloodlust and bonhomie so commingled!
   In England men grow old and fat and tired,
   Until there is no fight – except against
   The taxes – but here in France they seem to thrive
   Without regard to age, infirmity,
   Or redress. Perhaps we English suffer
   Some congenital blemish of obese ease
   Or from a surfeit of society.
   Whatever 'tis so exalts the Norman creed
   I cannot quite make out the surplus or
   The lack.
WILLIAM   What of my proposals, sir, or hath your
   Speech not closed?
HAROLD   I have said enough, my lord.
   You seek my allegiance – homage to
   Your lordship as his English vassal?
WILLIAM   I do,
   Sir, not as Duke of Normandy but as
   Thy future king.
HAROLD   And that king you well
   May be, if thy vassal's interest can secure it.
WILLIAM   I have your oath of fealty then?
   He gestures to bible
   The holy book is here: swear it.
HAROLD   I do
   You homage, sire.
WILLIAM   And wilt thou advocate
   For me before the Witan council?

HAROLD   I
   Have said as much, my lord.
WILLIAM   Say it again,
   Liegeman.
HAROLD   You have, sire, the promise of aught
   I can give you.
WILLIAM   And what of my daughter's hand?
HAROLD   May our rite of matrimony not long
   Follow thy coronation mass.
WILLIAM   Or better –
   May it precede. Rise, Earl Harold,
   My future son. As all of you bore witness,
   The earl did swear me fealty,
   And but reconfirmed the verity of my
   Succession to the English throne.
      He reveals reliquary
   Be these saintly relics the sacred seal
   Of that trust made here tonight.
      Murmurs
HAROLD   And in the spirit
   Of that trust, Duke William – now most devout –
   I beseech your lordship's leave to depart,
   With speed, for England. I have critical
   Dispatches and a summons from the king –
   Who only just learned of my presence here –
   Which, during the swift prosecution of
   This bold campaign, perforce have been ignored.
   They cannot be so longer.
WILLIAM *(aside to HAROLD)* We'll discuss
   This subject after the repast. *(Aloud, toasting)* For now
   It's time to eat and to forget our woes –
   To celebrate victory over foreign foes!
FITZ-OSBERN *(to servants)* Bring in the victuals, but no more ale.

Act I scene 6: England. Bosham Manor, Harold's home in Wessex.

Household servants pass busily over the stage. EDITH stands in a doorway.

EDITH   I lean and think on a threshold
   While the real work of being grunts
   And whistles past my door. I look up
   For a moment, as though a purpose'd come to mind,
   And then…but flick a speck from off my cloak.
     Enter HOSTLER, crossing the stage
   Is the courser's new saddle ready?
HOSTLER   Just about, madam – it only lacks a girth.* These
   horses all need stabling, though – I've got to make room.
     Exit HOSTLER
EDITH   Fear me – I fear me – wherefore comes this most
   Unsettling calm? – This unprovoked ennui,
   This deadness? Why am I so taciturn?
   Harold, my beloved earl whom I thought dead,
   Rides here today – arrives, dismounts, and kisses me –
   Him – my husband, would he be – my charmed
   And charming knight-at-arms, whom I most love,
   Most dearly.
     Enter SERVANT GIRL with garland and bouquet
SERVANT GIRL   Milady, I made a garland for you. Will you
   wear it?
     She offers garland
EDITH   No, thank you – I'll wear this diadem. Where do you
   go with those other flowers?
SERVANT GIRL   I had thought to dress the table with 'em.
EDITH   The table's well appointed – put some in the guest
   quarters and the rest in the chapel.
SERVANT GIRL   Yes, milady.

---

girth   band or strap usu. of leather passing under a horse's midsection by which a saddle is secured

Exit SERVANT GIRL
EDITH   For can I say I do not love,
   Esteem him my most loyal friend and councilor:
   Tenderest of allies, mildest of antagonists –
   Choicest minister – most cherished fool?
   Do I lie to say I love or is love
   Like the seasons and this an autumn time?
      Voice offstage: "His lordship's at the gate."
   What is that worn conceit? – What is fall
   To me but one part in a year, that year in fifty,
   Fifty in ten hundred thousand! I lie –
   I lie and shame myself with lying,
   With protesting…lies. I gall myself with my
   Ingratitude. It can't be helped. Ask me
   Whom I love? Or do not, for it sickens me.
   Who can know a heart too dear* for loving?
   Who can know such a man? Alas, I do.
      EDITH withdraws. Enter HAROLD.
HAROLD   Here, at home, finally my feet are grounded –
   Now, where's my enchantress t' lift them off
   Again?
EDITH *(coming forward)* What if my sorcery's died in
   Your absence?
HAROLD   It nothing has – I feel
   Light as wind in your presence.
EDITH   Then I
   Should rather brace you down.
      They embrace
HAROLD   Now it is over.
   When the sea choked and dragged me under –
   When the scaly shores conspired to scour me –
   When the blustering duke – whom we'll leave unnamed –
   Insulted and reviled both king and family,
   Laying siege with a catapult's finesse

dear grievous; severe

To the bastion of the English crown – when,
I say, through all this gauntlet I had run,
It was thought of country and the dream of you
That kept the blows from scoring. And now –
At last it's over. *(Pause)* Why so quiet Edith?

EDITH   I cannot say, my lord. Perhaps I am
Confused with thankfulness – for it was in
This moment comprised all my hopes for thee,
And here we are now living in it.

HAROLD   So, what
Comes next, Cassandra?*

EDITH   You go to London.

HAROLD   I do not believe you.

EDITH   And it's Edith,
Not Cassandra.

HAROLD   You know, you may be right –
I was thinking of a Norman lady.
   Enter EDWIN
(Aside to EDITH) More witchcraft!
(Aloud) My Lord of Mercia – welcome to Bosham!

EDWIN   Thank you, sire. I shan't stay long, however.

HAROLD   That is most unfortunate.

EDWIN   So is the news
I bear, my lord, but it is not fit for
Women's hearing.

HAROLD   What?! Not for these
Lovely lobes? Deliver us both your wretched
News, sir.

EDWIN   The king's delight at your
Survival brittles with the tempering* of northern

Cassandra (Greek mythology) granted prophetic powers by Apollo for her great beauty, when she refused his sexual advances he cursed her so that none would ever believe her predictions

tempering (metallurgy) process by which a metal such as steel is alternately heated and cooled to impart strength, toughness, or elasticity – if the metal is heated or cooled too quickly it can become brittle

Insurrectionists. Tostig's hold is lost,
He's fled, and a rebellious mob stomps
Toward London to demand consensus.
HAROLD   Consensus in what, Mercia?
And why does the king post you to tell me this?
EDWIN   The king had sent a courier, my lord,
But that I entreated for the task.
It was Morcar, sire, whom the elders and thegns chose
To succeed your ruthless brother.
HAROLD   And goes he with the rabble?
EDWIN   He refused, sire,
Though the overzealous thegns who joined
Did beg him.
HAROLD   I marvel at the fledgling's
Sudden circumspection. What does the king
Want I should do?
EDWIN   He demands you intercept
This lowborn force before it reaches Middlesex.*
HAROLD   And then?
EDWIN   Destroy it.
HAROLD   The king was enraged if he told you so.
But list: to speak ill of Tostig
I won't brook any sure opinion. Indeed,
There is the warrant of many desp'rate counts
Against him, luridly replete with horrors,
Extortions, ambush, and a charnel* more
Atrocity and vice that, were't even
Partly true, 'twould break the balance and bring
The tackle crashing down. But there's that
Popular exaggeration, too, morphs
A man unliked or enigmatical
Into a werewolf or a plague of monsters

Middlesex i.e. London
charnel building, room, or vault in which corpses or human bones are stored

For the real brutes to slay. And maugre* all
  He's still my brother, though I've long feared
  His violent caprices.
EDWIN　　　　　　　When will you
  Depart, my lord?
HAROLD　　　　　Where is this legion gone?
EDWIN　Scouts put them near Derby, but it is two
  Days since.
HAROLD *(to EDITH)* Shall I stay tonight or leave
  I' the morning?
EDITH　　　　　I should like both, my lord.
HAROLD　Wake me in the morning, Mercia, or
  Wilt thou not stay?
EDWIN　　　　　　I cannot – I will not –
  The king enjoined my most immediate return.
HAROLD　Did he? Derby, you say. *(To EDITH)* I can't tarry,
  Edith, I'm sorry. You make too fine
  A prophetess.
EDITH　　　　Derby closes fast
  On London, sire.
HAROLD　　　　　And so will I on you
  When this parley's* over.
EDITH　　　　　　　There'll be no fighting
  Then?
HAROLD　Not against these men, nor any
  Other thegns or drengs* so justifiably
  Aggrieved.
EDITH　　　Did he do what is suspected?
HAROLD　I don't know, Edith. *(He kisses her)* You'll see me
  anon.

  　　　Exeunt HAROLD and EDWIN. Enter SERVANT GIRL.
SERVANT GIRL　The master's leaving?

---

maugre　(archaic) in spite of
parley　meeting under truce between enemies to discuss terms
dreng　peasant landowner of Northumbria

EDITH *(handing SERVANT GIRL diadem)* Yes – *(Exit SERVANT GIRL)* while I remain...with my childish conceits.

Act I scene 7: London. The king's great hall on Thorney Island.

AELDRED is assisting EDWARD, who lies on the floor near his throne with papers strewn about him which the clerk is collecting. The chamberlain is also present. Housecarls stand guard.

AELDRED   Your highness? My lord?
EDWARD   Oh, I've fallen.
AELDRED   No – you did not fall. Some malady took your reason, just as at the abbey.
EDWARD   It was a fall, Archbishop. Oh, if I wore coarser garments –
AELDRED   Do you mean to say that –
EDWARD   Horsehair,* perhaps.
AELDRED   Chamberlain, has the king's bed been dressed?
   Chamberlain comes forward
EDWARD   I will sit in the hall...though it is drafty...and cold. *(Chamberlain retires. After a pause, looking at papers.)* These hidage* assessments – are they uniform?
AELDRED   *(handing EDWARD more papers given him by the clerk)* You dropped the equivalence tables, sire, when you fell.
EDWARD   That may be. Yes. I was righteous and He smote me.
AELDRED   Hadn't you best retire, your majesty?
   Enter STIGAND
EDWARD   I do not like that man, Archbishop.
AELDRED   *(aside to EDWARD)* All Hallows is fleeting – he won't be here

---

horsehair a hair shirt or "cilice" was often worn esp. by monks to induce discomfort, either as a penance or as a symbol of atonement
hidage a property tax paid to the king

For long. *(Aloud)* Greetings, my southern counterpart,
How is thy flock?
STIGAND   Much the more peaceable,
I'm sure – they bear up well under my oppressive
Yoke. *(To EDWARD)* Most gracious sovereign – my most humble
Lord – in your exalted presence I quite
Forget my honors.
AELDRED   And, so it seems, does he.
EDWARD   Canterbury.
AELDRED   The king is rapt in state affairs, your grace.
EDWARD   No, I am not.
STIGAND   Then I shall return tomorrow at a time
More convenient to his purposes,
Your greatness.
   AELDRED draws STIGAND aside
AELDRED   Perhaps you could visit me
In my apartments – his highness is unwell.
STIGAND   Is he? I am loath to hear it. Grave news
Has reached my sees, the which I had with mournful
Tact informed the king: Wulfric, Abbot of
Saint Athelwines, is dead – a cleric of great
Distinction and friendly with his majesty.
AELDRED   Yes – he has borne these sorrowful tidings.
STIGAND   The abbot was a monk to marvel at –
I knew him well – by reputation – and often
Planned to visit him before he expired.
AELDRED   And I will gladly recollect for you
Tomorrow, Archbishop, the myriad of his
Saintly qualities – even to thaumaturgy* –
But today the king is indisposed
And I must wait upon him.
STIGAND *(closely)* The security of the abbotship
Concerns me, your excellence.

thaumaturgy   term used to describe the miracles performed by saints

AELDRED By security you mean succession?
STIGAND A wise inference, excellency,
   But the truth, your grace, does not appall me.
   If I am greedy, greatness, then, as I've
   Been anointed both holy and a man,
   Pronounce me avaricious for the Lord.
AELDRED Archbishop –
STIGAND   But will you broach it with him?
AELDRED Tomorrow, Archbishop. God be with you.
STIGAND And with you. Until our conclave* – not the blessing – that may continue. And God bless you, your highness, my ever-loving liege.
   Exit STIGAND
EDWARD The consecration will be soon.
AELDRED The work wants a few weeks, but yes, sire, it
   will be.
EDWARD If I had made that pilgrimage.
AELDRED The abbey stands as testament to your
   Innumerable deeds of piety,
   Not one unfortunate omission.
EDWARD He will profane the rite.
AELDRED I will carry out the consecration,
   But Canterbury will be present – there is
   No helping that.
EDWARD *(to himself)* Had I lived, perhaps: a horsehair pilgrimage. But my words are swallowed up. Yes. Is there any taste in the white of an egg?* *(After a pause, aloud)* Where is the hearth boy?
   Enter HAROLD
HAROLD My worthy king! It is good to see you,
   Your highness. Your excellency, well met –
   I'd never thought I so could miss

---

conclave private or secret meeting; the confidential meeting of Catholic cardinals for the purpose of electing a new pope
But my words…an egg? See Job 6:3, 6:6 (King James Version, as all further biblical references)

The courts and baileys,* the walls and cavernous halls
Of Thorney Island!
AELDRED *(greeting him)* The king is much relieved
You are restored to him – as am I.
HAROLD   Your majesty seems most subdued today.
EDWARD   I am ill and shan't get well.
HAROLD   I hope that you exaggerate, my lord –
I have heard nothing of any illness.
EDWARD   It is true.
HAROLD   Can it be so hopeless? Are you certain?
EDWARD   Perhaps I shall rally.
HAROLD   Shouldn't you rest, my lord, to aid in your
Recovery?
EDWARD   I am feeling much better. Archbishop.
   EDWARD whispers to AELDRED
AELDRED *(aside to HAROLD)* The king is weary with discussion of
His health. He has had some one or two brief
Episodes of fainting that he'd prefer
We all ignore. *(Aloud)* Therefore, if it please you,
Resolve us both upon your confrontation
With the rebels of Northumbria.
For my part, as I am steward to that see,*
And often truant – for his majesty –
I fear my own neglectfulness may've hastened
This breach into a torrent.
HAROLD   Archbishop, no blame in this is yours –
Tostig ruled without forethought, subtlety,
Or discretion, heaping tax on tallage,
Dues and rents on imposts and banalities.*
He levied, billeted, and by all manner

---

bailey outer courtyard of a castle or stronghold
as I am steward to that see the city of York, Archbishop Aeldred's cathedral seat, was located in Northumbria
tallage…imposts and banalities fees of various sorts that could be forced by powerful lords upon manorial tenants and freeholders

And means exhausted the people's sympathy
Like a coal clamp.* It was their love for you,
Your majesty, th't kept them smoldering
So long beneath the sammel instead of
Blasting off the cap of it.*
EDWARD *(to AELDRED)*   What is sammel?
HAROLD   When I met the rebels on a knoll
In Oxfordshire, they said as much as this –
And more – accusing him of outrages
So hellish they should have no name, no sound,
No comprehension. And yet, of all these
Blacknesses but one – a single damning act –
Illumined witness ere it guttered out:
Kenrick, the Thegn of Easingwold, was murdered
In the street by Tostig – by my brother –
They had men there that saw it done.
   Pause
AELDRED *(consoling HAROLD)* Thou art truly noble, Harold
   Godwinson,
And serve thy state and kingdom like an host
Of angels – what man could fly with thee?
HAROLD   I have betrayed my brother, Aeldred, and
   I fear for him.
AELDRED   You must forget him as
   A brother and fear his ungovernable nature.
EDWARD   I fear a civil war, Archbishop.
HAROLD   No, mine humble lord, there'll be no war,
   Though you won't, at first, be pleased with the sequel
   To my encounter. Whether there be truth
   Or no in any other infamy lain
   Against the ousted earl, his subjects will

coal clamp   conically arranged pile of wood with a central flue, covered with earth or clay, then allowed to slowly burn (or, more precisely, to "char") over several days yielding charcoal, which burns at a much higher temperature than wood and was used to fuel forges and kilns
sammel...cap of it   sammel is a clayey subsoil that was often used to cover a coal clamp; after a clamp was fired via the central flue, the flue was plugged or "capped" to prevent total combustion of the wood

Not have him back. When I threatened them
With force of far more potent arms
And soldiery, they only paused a moment,
Then, redoubling their defiance, thrust up
Their picks and mattocks* higher, bristling the hilltop,
And uttered such concerted whoops and shouts
As'd startle Morpheus* from slumber.
Enter HEARTH BOY

AELDRED How ends the quarrel? Did you beat them back
Or yield?
HEARTH BOY gives HAROLD a note

HAROLD I told them Morcar would be earl
If your majesty would have him. *(To HEARTH BOY)* Thank you.
He reads note then glances out a nearby window
He was not among the treasoners – should
You so see them – and I could not attack
Countrymen so wholly victimized
By blood of mine.

AELDRED Your majesty? My liege? Sire?!
EDWARD, briefly dazed, now recovers. AELDRED whispers
with him then motions to clerk, who approaches. To clerk.
Go to the chancery – have a writ drawn
Banishing the former earl and confiscating
His estates. Bring it here when 'tis done.
He writes something then hands the paper to clerk
And deliver this to the Earl of Mercia
Where he lodges in the city – he will be
Expecting it.
Exit clerk

HAROLD What of the men who bide
In Oxford?

AELDRED Of them –

---

mattock tool shaped like a pickaxe but with one end broad like an adze instead of pointed
Morpheus (Greek mythology) the god of dreams

EDWARD   – the king will speak.
  Earl of Wessex, it is God's will that those men be spared.
HAROLD   God's will and a gentle king's.
EDWARD   For egg whites plow iniquity.
HAROLD   My lord?
    EDWARD tries to speak but manages only jargon, then collapses
AELDRED   Attendants! Bring a litter* – his highness is ill!
HAROLD   I will hold you, my lord.
EDWARD   *(seeing HEARTH BOY)* Hearth-bluck-wuck-g-g-g-goy-hoy-doy-b-b-b-b-b-boy.
HAROLD   Yes, that's right.

Act I scene 8: London. The southern shore of the Thames, almost directly across from Thorney Island.

TOSTIG addresses HAROLD, who is offstage. There are a few trees scattered about.

TOSTIG   Well, Dei Gratia, Dux Anglorum* –
  How was Flanders? Did you see our kinsmen?
  Practice longer strokes – you are out of breath.
    HAROLD pulls the bow of a dinghy within view and enters, breathing heavily
HAROLD   The ship miscarried – I was wrecked in France.
  It is good to see you, Tostig, but the king –
  Edward – has been seized by some distemper –
  I can't stay long.
TOSTIG   Nor can I since banished by my brother.
    Pause

---

litter a bed or couch suspended between shafts and carried by two or more people
Dei Gratia, Dux Anglorum (Latin) "By the grace of God, leader of the English" – style of address combined with an honorific title; both were granted Harold by the king in recognition of his service

HAROLD It's been almost fifteen years since we banked our longships on this shore –
TOSTIG Well, so it has.
HAROLD – Drank and supped here in our mail shirts, whilst father worked the peace.
TOSTIG Yes – I remember well enough: the tide gone out and the masts unstepped.* I stood on a thwart* as we wafted upriver, under the mobs at London Bridge –
HAROLD – That flung out garlands on us, don't forget. And then we came unto this place.
TOSTIG And father worked the peace – yes, I know. Who will work it this time, Harold?
HAROLD What would you have me do, Tostig?
Can I reverse the order of your murders
And undo them? Restore the mothers
To their children, the husbands to their wives,
The fathers to their families? Tell me –
You must tell me – how much of this
Is true and how much my own sophistry?*
TOSTIG It's all true if you believe it or nothing If you don't.
HAROLD   No riddles, Tostig.
I know you killed the Thegn of Easingwold.
TOSTIG Only when he drew on me and attacked.
HAROLD You are banished from the kingdom but not
By me – petty device and the megrims*
That distort your actions breed this harsh exile,
Force it on you like a blasted* child.
TOSTIG How tidy you make the swine pit!
HAROLD Go to Flanders, Tostig – but be careful
In your crossing. Pay the wergild,* and go –

---

unstep remove (a mast) from its support mount or socket
thwart crosspiece forming a seat on a boat
sophistry plausible but fallacious reasoning or argumentation
megrim (archaic) capricious notion; whim
blasted disfigured by disease
wergild payment made to a murder victim's family as restitution and to avoid possible reprisals

Restore yourself to honor.
TOSTIG And then what?!
No. I'll take back what is mine.
HAROLD And I
Will back the sons of Aelfgar* in that conflict –
Our two clans must guard against division
Lest forces outside strike us through the cleft.
TOSTIG That idea seems pat enough. I knew
You'd not support me – it wouldn't serve
To be more brotherly.
   Pause
HAROLD Do you recall that time in the whitewater above
the falls, when we nearly lost his best surcoat.*
TOSTIG What are you trying to say?
HAROLD I held your hand to fish it out.
TOSTIG You wax sentimental, Harold – we were boys.
HAROLD Do I? You could've killed me here,
Yet I came.
TOSTIG Out of slavish filiation –
You're still jessed* to his rotting arm.
HAROLD Indeed.
Get thee to Flanders, Tostig.
TOSTIG You came here like a governess to scold me.
HAROLD I came because you asked!
   Exit HAROLD pulling dinghy. TOSTIG yells after him.
TOSTIG Do you need a hand now, Subregulus?!*
What, man?! What do you need?!
   He plucks a leafy twig off a nearby tree
Here: to freshen your laurels...

sons of Aelfgar Edwin and Morcar
surcoat loose-fitting tunic worn over armor
jess short leather strap fastened to each leg of a raptor and used to secure the bird to a leash or to tether it to the hand (properly "fist" or "glove") of the falconer
Subregulus another of Harold's honorifics

Act I scene 9: Normandy. Grounds of the duke's castle in Rouen.

Enter ROB and WILL

ROB   And the English chevaliers, if they be tricked by elves to chew upon a certain root, then, when the dark's come, they scream most wretchedly and all their skin peels off.
WILL   But we have elves.
ROB   Not so mean as these wights.*
WILL   They could spit out the root.
ROB   By then it can't be helped – but, should they climb into a pool afore the prime* then they'll scream again but grow new skin, and so must they every night.
WILL   What if they do not find the pools?
ROB   Then stay they skeletons forever and don thick cowls to hide themselves.
WILL   Can't they be cured? *(Pause)* Thou'd try to frighten me – it's a lie.
ROB   Boy, don't call me liar! *(Cuffs WILL, who starts to cry)* I would it were not true. Be quiet. But there's more that's even worse than this to tell: all the time there, William – be it even to an hundred moons – thou must wear a handkerchief over thine eyes, and knowest why?
WILL   No.
ROB   If thou be not born there, thou must is all.
WILL   But how shall I cross a bridge, or choose my food? I will get lost there, Robert.
ROB   And likely fall into a well betimes,* like many another Norman lord who've done the same, clogging English wells all over rather than be murdered. That's the trouble of it, I suppose, though thou might'st peak a little through

wight   [1] (archaic) human being [2] (obsolete) supernatural creature or spirit
prime   first of the seven canonical hours, just after sunrise
betimes   (archaic) in a short time; soon

the fabric, and also use a stick. But beware thou, keep thy kerchief up so the English stay plain with 'ee, for if it fall or even give a slip and thou look'st on them with just one part of an eye and they cast straight at thee, well, after that they'll keep on seeming plain, but behind their friendly looks they'll be secreting how to kill thee.

WILL Well, they are cowards then. *(Enter WILLIAM)* Sire, must the dogs wear little kerchiefs too?

WILLIAM What are you talking about, boy?

WILL When we go to England –

WILLIAM *(to ROB, ignoring WILL)* Who spoke to you of there?

ROB I only heard the king is sick, my lord, and soon dead.

WILLIAM From whom?

ROB I'm not sure, my lord.

WILL Sire –

WILLIAM *(ignoring WILL)* Short-boot,* wilt thou join the next hunt with thy father?

ROB Yes, my lord, if you'll allow it.

WILLIAM I shall not hunt with a blathering child – be mindful. And rule thy brother, do not trifle with him.

WILL Sire – thou wilt be king in England.

WILLIAM What of it?

WILL When thou art king –

WILLIAM Aye, when – and then we'll talk on it. Now get about some useful piece of business.

Exit WILLIAM

ROB Go on then, get about it.

WILL *(teasing)* Yes, my lord, if –

ROB *(cuffing WILL)* You be quiet.

WILL If you'll allow it.

Exit WILL running with ROB chasing after

Short-boot derisive nickname given by the duke to his son

Act I scene 10: England. Bosham Manor. The bakehouse.

FREYA is making bread at a table. EDITH lends some assistance.

FREYA He softened some after did the Dane king* – but he was sorely grieved and in a fit eftsoons* he brung his throne down near the sea and bid the waves haste t' take him out, or so 'twas said – that day was wheat and rye. No, it weren't winter when she drowned – when I found her stark there 'gainst the sluices* – sorry madam – there was little flowers up on the banks with birds among 'em. No, it was later 'n now – warmer – but that water was sure acold – and she – well – it was a barley day – yes, barley – though the Dane ate none, or after e'en. Girls is so curious madam. She was a good 'n too.

EDITH I'd bethought myself to warm here, Freya,
By the ovens and thy cheerful company,
But instead I find me chilled and saddened.
What puts you in such a somber mood?
I'm used to far more sun and smiles from you –
Far less gloom leavening your histories.

FREYA Well, so – I am sad then. The new king's being sick puts me in mind o' the old 'uns, and that his majesty Canute did often visit here t' see his friend the earl th't he bestowaled it on,* though after he did ne'er stay the night. Then was your Earl Harold just a boy. What'll happen, madam, if this King Edward dies? There's some say Harold'll be king – 'n if he is then I'll be happy that he's crowned but also then afear for that what's next – for Freya 'n 'er 'usban' – for these ovens even 'n the mill, and

---

Dane king Canute, son of King Svein Forkbeard of Denmark, conquered England and ruled there 1016-1035
eftsoons (archaic) soon after; presently
sluice i.e. sluice gate, a wooden barrier set in grooves which is used to control the flow of a millrace or other waterway
earl th't he bestowaled it on Godwin of Wessex, the father of Harold and Tostig, who rose to prominence in the service of King Canute

you madam besides.
EDITH Oh Freya – King Edward may yet live –
And Harold: no one here in Bosham should
Take fear. All the worst contingencies,
The most unlikely 'coulds' and 'woulds' an anxious
Mind might dream up have been envisaged
By the earl. This is his home too,
My dear, and not quake nor cataclysm else,
Howsoe'er it's severe, could keep him,
In his heart or breath, much long away.
FREYA I'm sorry t' brood, madam – you're right, I ween,* on that. The earl's good – for a man – and they be often just a trouble.
 Enter TOSTIG disguised as a villager, carrying some articles
TOSTIG Where shall I set these down, dowager?
FREYA How's that? – Dowager?!
TOSTIG Thou art not a gentlewoman? A rich widow?
FREYA My 'usban' lives – 'n I serve the earl.
TOSTIG Apologies to them both. This must be thy grand-daughter – she is most beautiful.
FREYA She is my mistress. Get ye gone, scoundrel, before –
TOSTIG – Aye, that's the common theme.
EDITH How came you hither, sir?
TOSTIG By way of the gate, the longhouse, the hostler,
And the mill bridge.
EDITH   What is your purpose here?
TOSTIG To see the sun.
EDITH   The sun shows anywhere.
TOSTIG When she travels, i'faith – yes – but nowhere
Else so radiant.
EDITH   Freya, beat this man
With your peel.*

---

ween (archaic) suppose
peel shovel-like implement with a long handle used by bakers to move bread, pastries, etc. into and out of an oven

FREYA I'll not beat a lord, madam, though many times he
   did earn it.
      TOSTIG removes disguise
TOSTIG But which time most, Freya?
FREYA I don't know, sire.
TOSTIG But you do – though I was often nasty.
FREYA You was – and you was sometimes good.
TOSTIG I am not now – not either.
EDITH I will watch the ovens, Freya.
FREYA I'll take t' dinner then.
TOSTIG Good day, Freya.
FREYA Good day.
      Exit FREYA
TOSTIG I frightened her, but she's a sweet old dame.
   Heard you? – Harold is engaged.
EDITH   I had it
   In a letter – and then he told me so
   Himself – here – ere Christmas, with many
   Another thing besides, accounting for
   His seeming rashness.
TOSTIG   Tell me more –
   I long to hear it.
EDITH Do you? There were wars he had to join,
   Mockings to endure, oaths enforced
   Upon him – and all at the pleasure
   Of a wolvish duke.
TOSTIG   Wolvish – got you that
   From him? They sound more his words than thine.
EDITH Why are you here now, Tostig? I
   Had looked for you weeks ago, when Harold
   First wrote me of your banishment.
TOSTIG   Yes,
   I am tardy. I remained in London
   Mustering support.

EDITH   And flouting the decree.
   What if you were taken?
TOSTIG   The king knew of
   My presence there – between deliriums –
   Though not, I dare say, of my enterprise.
EDITH   What is this smugness – this complacency?
TOSTIG   Is it smug to purpose as I please?
EDITH   Are all murderers so dull-witted as this?
   These are my words now, Tostig:
   I know what desp'rate things you've done – you –
   Abhorrent, hateful things. Is there so much
   Malice in you – the wound so deep
   You'd gash it further till it teem with rot?
TOSTIG   There'll be no shame – I'll do what I must.
EDITH   What, Tostig – tell me – what supplication
   Will avail – what detrench this rancor?
   Would you have us hate you? You won't succeed.
   You'll only make us loathe ourselves.
   And when I speak to you know this: I speak
   As of a world of three – my whole world is –
   There's no Bosham in't, no Sussex, no England –
   'Tis thee – Harold, Edith, and Tostig, his hands
   Even reeking with gore. And still would you be –
   Brother of Harold, son of Godwin, beloved
   Of this same Edith – still I tell you though
   I'd slung the heads of mine own kinsmen
   On the pyre.
      Pause
TOSTIG   What will you make of me, lady?
   Or what shall I to you? This place –
   The people in't – I confuse –
   Of what worth are they – am I?
   What is my estate and reckoning here,
   There being nowhere else? It is not – nothing –

Void with a simple.* I exist for your
Exoneration – to shamble* your despairs
Mine make colossal strides.
EDITH Tostig, what are they?
TOSTIG   I will not say more.
Ride with me to the harbor. Nay,
Let us walk.
   Pause
EDITH Your brother – I know he spoke to you –
He was rueful at the way you parted.
TOSTIG And you do your duty by him.
EDITH My duty's done for both your loves.
TOSTIG   Yes –
I wonder at it.
EDITH   Is there any other way?
TOSTIG I don't know. Shall we walk?
EDITH   I must tend
The ovens…till the dowager returns.

Act I scene 11: London. Thorney Island. The king's bedchamber.

Nighttime. ROBERT sits next to a bed by a small window reading aloud from the bible, Isaiah 62:9 – 62:12. EDWARD lies on the bed, unconscious. The QUEEN is asleep in a chair.

ROBERT "…Sought out, a city not forsaken."
As my limbs are, or any attendant
Feeling in them. If I could only bring
My charger in – I'd declaim from the saddle –

---

simple [1] single and/or fundamental component of something esp. one that is unanalyzable
[2] (archaic) fool, simpleton
shamble i.e. make to shamble; also, playing on "shambles," a scene or state of devastation

That might be enough to rouse you! *(Pause)* Outside
Is cool and fair, my lord – the moon is out –
Recalls for me that night in the streambed
When we were lost, and a roebuck leapt overhead.
You, sire, were silent as that leap
In your regard of it, but I knew
You understood it – could make it God's again.
I should return.
    He resumes reading through 63:3
"…and I will stain all my raiment."
That sounds an awful mess, your highness –
How 'bout we play at merels?*
    The king's sleep becomes agitated
Sire?! My lord? Do your eyes open? It is
Your friend, Fitz-Wimark.

EDWARD *(awakening)*   My eldest of friends.

ROBERT Yes, it is. My king awakes. I know
Not what to do – I am caught in a brake!

EDWARD Close the casement, Robert – but not all the way.

ROBERT *(adjusting window)* Would you like some water, majesty – or viands?

EDWARD I will drink from the cup of the Lord, Robert.

ROBERT Will it be soon?

EDWARD *(looking around room)* It is conceivable.

ROBERT They are all without the chamber. Have you the strength to receive them, your grace?

EDWARD Perhaps. The queen – is in Wherwell?

ROBERT Oh dear, I had forgot – she's here, asleep – I'll wake her. *(Waking QUEEN)* Your majesty – the king is awake. Look.

QUEEN Oh, I am pleased – you are such a good king.

EDWARD You aren't in the nunnery?

QUEEN No, my lord – you had me back. It has been many years.

merels popular medieval board game

EDWARD Methinks* I remember. *(To ROBERT)* The queen has been as a beloved daughter to us – may God reward her service.
QUEEN That is very kind of you, my lord.
EDWARD Will they come, Robert?
ROBERT Right away, sire.
  Exit ROBERT. Pause.
QUEEN You look very well, my lord. Shall I comb your hair?
  Reenter ROBERT with AELDRED
AELDRED *(taking EDWARD's hand)* This is beyond all measure of hope!
EDWARD Yes. Is the consecration –
AELDRED   Gone past,
  My lord, it is gone past, but your pledge is kept –
  The congregants astound at your beneficence.
EDWARD You will take me there?
AELDRED In good time, my lord, of course.
EDWARD It will be soon, Archbishop.
  Enter HAROLD and HEARTH BOY
HAROLD   My gracious king,
  'Twas only in these last late hours that,
  From token of your restless sleep, our hopes
  Themselves bestirred. Praise be to God!
EDWARD *(aside to HAROLD)* Are the people happy?
HAROLD *(aside to EDWARD)* All is right in the realm.
EDWARD *(aside to HAROLD)* You will be a good king.
HAROLD *(aside to EDWARD)* The Witenagemot* awaits your word.
  Enter STIGAND
STIGAND Thrice gracious and heroic liege, we all
  Amaze at this miraculous continuation!
EDWARD Canterbury.
  Enter EDWIN and MORCAR

methinks (archaic) It seems to me
Witenagemot aka Witan Council (see note on pg 9)

AELDRED Here is the Earl of Mercia, and his
   Brother earl – of Northumbria.
EDWIN   May your
   Grace's health take nutriment from the country's
   New-sown peace.
MORCAR   I hope you are soon well,
   Your majesty.
EDWARD *(to MORCAR)* The old earl was less courteous.
MORCAR I have heard it said, your majesty.
EDWARD I am old.
MORCAR Yes – no – I don't know, your majesty.
EDWIN Morcar is not yet accustomed to your
   Majesty's manner – please forgive him.
EDWARD *(ignoring EDWIN)* Did you know him?
MORCAR Myself, sire?
   EDWIN pulls MORCAR away
EDWARD It is hard – to know oneself – especially for – *(Seeing
   HEARTH BOY)* There you are. *(Motions to HEARTH BOY, who
   approaches)* Fetch me some water.
HEARTH BOY Yes, your majesty.
EDWARD It is late. You will come back?
HEARTH BOY Straight away, your majesty.
   *Exit HEARTH BOY, returning soon after with a goblet of water,
   which he brings to EDWARD*
EDWARD   Oh Archbishop, I had forgot: I dreamed! Along
   the way to St. Aubert's in my shroud, Gervais and Alenard
   came and stopped me in the path.
ROBERT The Benedictines!*
EDWARD Yes, Robert. They sat me on a stone which was
   very cold – anon* I had my mantle – and told how, for all
   the wickedness in England, a year and one day hence

Benedictines monks belonging to the Benedictine Order, a Roman Catholic order of independent monastic communities observing the Rule of St. Benedict
anon (archaic) at once

angels with swords of forked lightning would come to
lay waste the land until a certain tree, felled halfway up
the trunk and the top cast three furlongs off, should rejoin
without aid and sprout new leaves again.
AELDRED   Your dream is most ominous, my lord.
QUEEN   They were always kindly monks.
HAROLD *(aside to STIGAND)* What import would you derive?
STIGAND *(aside to HAROLD)*   Oh,
I am an acolyte* again to hear
Our sometime Solomon descant in such
A sickly rave. Alack. But gentle earl,
Do not let these vengeful angels nor their
Horrid trees unnerve you. English wickedness –
At least in Kent, much of Sussex, Hampshire,
And Essex south of Alban's town – is straitened
Under Canterbury's watch – for I am
As another Draco* with my charges.
AELDRED *(aside to HAROLD)* The king's vision hath a weird truth in it.
HAROLD *(aside to AELDRED)* And when he dreamt he was a stool?
AELDRED *(aside to HAROLD)* That was most curious.
HAROLD *(aside to AELDRED)*   As much as I
Do love the king, that end itself is love,
And cannot be idolatry.
To grant this apparition's simulacrum,
Even, to the truth would do dishonor
To that love and shamefully bring me down
From it.
AELDRED *(aside to HAROLD)* Well – but Numbers Twelve doth say* –

---

acolyte altar boy; a usu. young member of the Catholic Church who assists a cleric in the performance of liturgical rites
Draco Ancient Athenian legislator remembered primarily for his notoriously harsh law code
Numbers Twelve 12:6 "If there be a prophet among you, I the Lord will make myself known unto him in a vision, and will speak unto him in a dream."

EDWARD Soon I shall not dream anymore – instead, I shall die *(QUEEN starts to cry)* – and be dead. *(QUEEN wails)* But you mustn't mourn for me. Pray for my soul – that I die softly – up to heaven – and the Lord not over-scourge me for being royal.
AELDRED God would never scourge such an innocent.
EDWARD Wessex, come and take my hand.
HAROLD Yes, my king.
EDWARD This woman and the rest of my kingdom are hereby given over into your protection. You must try to be righteous as I have been, take care of Robert, and listen to the archbishop. When I die, do not conceal it – tell them all, that they may pray God's mercy on a humble sinner.
HAROLD I will do just as you ask, my lord.
EDWARD I would rest awhile – alone – but just a short while, and then you may return.
HAROLD Yes, my lord.
EDWIN *(to HAROLD)* Shall I inform the remainder of the council? Though it be midnight, the Witan will convoke.
AELDRED *(overhearing)* Go Mercia, but take Fitz-Wimark with you.
ROBERT Your excellency, I should like to stay near my friend.
AELDRED Of course – so should I.
STIGAND *(overhearing)* Then I will board this solemn delegation. My Lord of Mercia, lead on!
  Exeunt EDWIN, MORCAR, and STIGAND at one side, and HAROLD, AELDRED, ROBERT, and HEARTH BOY opposite. Pause.
QUEEN It is often quiet here, but not tonight.
EDWARD Tonight is very different – not usual.
QUEEN You slept for many days, my lord – you must feel rested.
EDWARD No, I do not.
QUEEN I darned some mittens for the chamberlain – he is

very pleasant. Can I get you soup, my lord? In the morning the cook will boil some eggs – you like eggs. So do I. Eggs are so good – with salt.

EDWARD   Yes – with salt.

QUEEN   Shall I comb your hair?

EDWARD   Archbishop!

Act II scene 1: London. Somewhere in Westminster Abbey.

Enter HAROLD, crowned

HAROLD But 'king' is a word: the king died yesterday –
Thou art king today. And how, Harold?
By vivats* and regalia? How
But by fortuity – because the atheling*
Is a boy. Where's divinity in that?!
But this is bitter reverence.
   Pause
A word – a monarch overwhelms a word,
Speeches, whole histories – even one
Too meek to rule. And 'tis the Lord appoints thee,
Harold – makest thee His sacred vassal
Through the Witan's homely agency.
There is no chance in it – 'n can only be
That in our savior's wondrous-arced design,
Till Doomsday England's, and now my, fated
Arrow fly together at the target.
   Pause
So say who am I? The grandson of a churl.*
I have no Cerdic* blood. Even so, I
Am king. And William's claim, the predicate
Of forcèd oaths? Dismissed like a page – renounced –
O'erthrown. Through ceremonies unconstrained
Am I anointed, crowned, and triple sworn.*
All that remains is to serve.
   Enter EDWIN

---

vivat (Latin) "Long may he/she live" – traditional exclamation, often followed by "Rex" or "Regina," shouted by commoners in support of a newly crowned monarch
atheling Anglo-Saxon prince or nobleman, esp. a kingdom's heir apparent
churl peasant; member of the lowest class of freemen in Anglo-Saxon society
Cerdic founder of an early Saxon dynasty from which almost all subsequent Anglo-Saxon kings – Harold being a notable exception – claimed ancestry
triple sworn the new king vowed to defend the Church, preserve the peace, and rule over the people mercifully

EDWIN   Your majesty.
HAROLD   My Earl of Mercia,
   What joy is it beams in your face?! – I am
   Utterly blinded.
EDWIN   Yet your gibe aims straight.
   I lack the habit of your wonted mirth,
   As well you know.
HAROLD   Indeed I do. The news.
EDWIN   Even now he rages up the Kentish coast,
   Marauding recklessly to keep his crews
   Provisioned.
HAROLD *(aside)* Brother, you find me my humility.
   (Aloud) Call out the fyrd* in Lindsey. Have Morcar
   Do the same north of the Humber.
EDWIN   And when
   He comes?
HAROLD   Drive him off from there. *(Pause)* Mercia.
EDWIN   Your majesty?
HAROLD   Let him go.
EDWIN   This wayward man is too
   Dangerous to live.
HAROLD   No more dangerous
   Than Aelfgar was when, outlawed, he allied
   With Gruffydd to invade us.
EDWIN   Nor more
   Than Godwin, sire, when he and his defied
   The writ.
HAROLD   It seems we've all been miscreant.
   Tostig is my brother – I will not say:
   "Destroy him."
EDWIN   Is cautery destruction?
   Was my brother so traitorous –
HAROLD   Go on.

---

fyrd   militia; army of freemen, each of whom was expected to provide his own arms and provisions

EDWIN Though such a thing's impossible – I would
  Forfeit him without compunction.
HAROLD   Forfeit him
  O'er whose nurturance you've had such constant scope?
  There's no need here to say such things.
EDWIN   I hope
  He'd do the same for me.
HAROLD   Very well then:
  So do I.
EDWIN *(bowing)* Your highness.
  Exit EDWIN
HAROLD Tender fratricide. But what shall I do?
  Am I made king for this? To murder my
  Own brother – or worse – to have it done by hire.
  Shall I take an army there myself
  And beg him from the van? And if he'd fight?
  Then Abel murders Abel – Tostig, there'll be
  No Cain.
  Hallo! Mercia, I trust too well in thy duty.
  Enter HOUSECARLS
  Send me a clerk and heralds.
HOUSECARLS   Yes, your majesty.
HAROLD Fly to it, friends!
  Exeunt HOUSECARLS
                He'd only kill you brother –
  Unless more noxious remedies present.

Act II scene 2: England. Bosham Manor.

Enter EDITH reading a letter, some of it aloud

~~~~~~

To the Mistress of Bosham,

    The world is drab while I am in it, or so it seems in this icy grayness – like a corpse. Am I dead? Is that the antiphon?* Why do we walk – strut – nay, storm the earth if we're only to sift apart?! I've done dastard ill – it haunts me – I shall try not to do worse – but nothing slakes – no one – not you – nor could I wish it now that I am in the midst. I must punish my fortunes further – bind me to the wheel myself to go around.* But peace.

    You say he played no part in the revolt – perhaps it's true. I think on him withal – he should think more on you.

    We had a fine walk, did we not? – I hope you did not catch cold. Make these dull clouds depart, my lady, or shimmer with thy likeness – I cannot see your face.

    Written from shipboard at Hastings and entrusted, with boasts of your munificence, to a fisherman bound for Chichester.

– T.

~~~~~~

EDITH Why trudge it out again – why reread
    A thing so tortured and so moribund?
      She resumes reading
    But it breathes. Tostig, what do you mean
    To tell me? That you are sunk past saving?
    I won't believe it. Why do you despair?
    You had a cruel father – then why did it

---

antiphon short scriptural verse sung or recited responsively as part of the liturgy usu. before and after a canticle or psalm
bind me...go around conflating the metaphorical wheel of fortune with the breaking wheel, a torture device

Not blight you both? What hallow-headed goddess
Blessed thy brother but could not do the like
For thee? If I could carry children –
If I could raise them –
But there's too much sorrow over that.
Would my own mum had reared ye –
Though a lowly woman and infirm, yet…
There was love enough.
Harold – well – he tends an ailing king –
There's none who would reproach such somber duty –
And I'd see more of both – or –
What beggars possibility.
ROBERT *(offstage)*   – So many swallows
One could hawk the grounds here with a hobby.*
EDITH   Who is this jaunty fellow?
ROBERT *(offstage)*   Yes, so long.
   He enters
Pardon, madam – you are the Lady Edith –
The king unseeled* my swelling eyes with your
Description. I am Robert Fitz-Wimark, late
Of my King Edward's side – arrivèd here
To tell you –
EDITH   That Harold is now king.
ROBERT Yes, milady.
EDITH   And I'm to journey back
   With you.
ROBERT   What can be ill in this? Ah,
But he too had misgivings, or hesitance,
When first he called me to his royal presence.
He proposed that I, a noble mean
In learning, offer him what to be king was,
And if I thought there rectitude in such

---

hobby small falcon adept at catching prey on the wing
unseel (falconry) the eyes of a usu. young raptor were, in a former practice, sewn shut or "seeled" during the early stages of its training to make the bird more docile

Swift coronations. My liege, better to ask,
Said I, what steak from the unmaking.*
EDITH King Edward put great trust in you – and now,
I'm sure, does Harold. But was there rectitude?
ROBERT The bishops had not met again till Holy
Week. I do not think there was a choice.
Rightness though? I cannot speak to that.
Of what is right I only know the etiquette,
And not the way things sometimes will fall out.
EDITH Are you content with that?
ROBERT   No, madam,
But I will not strain to apprehend it either.
If I knew where the boar lay hid,
Or if his tusks would gore me,
Why would I hunt him?
But I am prey to grief. My thoughts stoop* down –
They are not natively devout.
EDITH I questioned you unfairly.
ROBERT   Did you?
The truth of it is my king is gone
And I will try to serve the new one.
EDITH Who would not judge that sentiment devout?
ROBERT Indeed? Then I shall memorize and craft
A speech from what I said. *(Pause)* Ah, now I've
Forgot!
EDITH You try too hard to remember –
Or deliberately to forget.
ROBERT   You are
More clever than I understand. Forgive me –
I know not how else to ask: may I
Lure* you to an unfair question?

unmaking (hunting) ritual butchery of a deer carcass at the conclusion of a hunt, involving the distribution of specific parts of the carcass to the hunt's participants in accordance with tradition and rank
stoop (falconry) to dive, as at prey
lure (falconry) to recall a bird from flight or when training it for quarry by swinging around a feathered decoy tied to a long cord

EDITH   Yes, sir –
  I believe I owe you an advantage.
ROBERT   Madam,
  What was't in hearing such fortunate news
  You seemed already to possess, th't yet
  Proved so upsetting?
EDITH   The king will give me o'er.
ROBERT How can you know this for a certainty?
EDITH Is the boar always where the hounds lead you?
ROBERT No, madam, not always.
EDITH   Then I may be wrong,
  Sir.
ROBERT I hope that you are.
EDITH   Robert Fitz-Wimark,
  You are an honest man.
ROBERT   Bah! Thou hast
  Not seen me ride!

Act II scene 3: Normandy. Grounds of the duke's castle in Rouen.

Enter ODO and several Norman NOBLES followed by FITZ-OSBERN, WILLIAM, and ROB. All are in hunting dress and some are also carrying gear and weapons.

NOBLE 4   If not your bow 'twould be your saddle, if not your saddle 'twould be your breaches – from breaches thence to boots, from boots out to spurs, and spurs to flanks till all blame escape thee into thy horse!
NOBLE 5   Certainly I shall make no excuses for you!
NOBLE 4   Nor should you undertake to – it were a task insurmountable for one who can hardly board his nag.
NOBLE 5   Must be all that buggering keeps you so trim. Could I induce you to disclose your regimen? – After the hunt,

perhaps, behind the stables?
NOBLE 4 I'll tell thee now – there's no slop in it, swine.
NOBLE 5 But plenty of warm milk, I'll wager.
NOBLE 4 In the muck with you.
    NOBLE 4 wrestles with NOBLE 5, who eventually throws him down
NOBLE 6 Bishop, it's not Sunday so I'll confess it in subjunctive: I may shoot a man today.
ODO Tell me which one, sir, lest we shoot the same.
NOBLE 6 You take Nimrod,* I'll the fat one – my aim's poor.
NOBLE 5 *(sitting on NOBLE 4)* How 'bout an oink, piglet?!
WILLIAM Quiet, the lot of you. *(To NOBLE 4 & 5)* Get up there! *(Presenting ROB)* Don't lean boy. Looks he formidable?
NOBLE 5 Oh, yes.
NOBLE 4 Absolutely.
NOBLE 6 Like a child Hercules!
WILLIAM Fitz-Osbern, what think you?
FITZ-OSBERN A little pale, perhaps, but a strong lad – he'll bear up.
WILLIAM The hunt'll bloody thy sallow face. Art ready?
ROB I think so.
    Enter SERVANT
WILLIAM Don't think – know thy purpose.
ROB Yes, my lord. I am ready.
WILLIAM Thy father's flask?
ROB On my – on the horse, sire.
WILLIAM Put it 'round thy neck. *(To SERVANT)* Where's the huntsman?
SERVANT My lord, I do not know – I am come from the castle.
WILLIAM Go on, then – what does she want?
SERVANT Your pardon, the news I bear is from England. King Edward's life has ended – Earl Harold is raised to the kingdom.

Nimrod [1] mighty hunter in biblical tradition [2] silly or foolish person

Pause. Exit WILLIAM.
FITZ-OSBERN *(to SERVANT)* Who else knows of this?
SERVANT   Word is all about the city, my lord.
FITZ-OSBERN *(to all)* The duke will not hunt today. *(To ROB)*
   Your deer will wait.
   Exeunt

Act II scene 4: Normandy. Within the duke's castle.

WILLIAM sits alone on a bench. Coats-of-arms and a family tapestry hang upon a wall.

WILLIAM   Where's the blood in me? – Drawn off –
   And the rest – skewered on a filthy spit
   The ruck turns.
   Pause. He rises and violently throws something.
   Rage split me – carve me t' the core! *(Sotto voce)* Murder
   The man'kinside* there, shrieking through the guts!
   Enter FITZ-OSBERN
FITZ-OSBERN   My lord, you must take action – Rouen consumes
   With the intelligence.
WILLIAM   Let them burn withal.
FITZ-OSBERN   And the courts of Europe that will scoff at
   And despise you? Put a kingly aspect
   On this ire –
WILLIAM   And subjugate the stars?*
   How?!
FITZ-OSBERN   Embolden your anger – exceed the news.
WILLIAM   Don't mystify – give me your meaning.
   I'll send ambassadors.

---

man'kinside   contraction of "manikin inside" with "manikin" understood as meaning a diminutive human being or homunculus
And subjugate the stars   William takes "aspect" in the astrological sense, referring to the relative positions of celestial bodies as exerting an influence on human affairs

FITZ-OSBERN   To what compulsion?
WILLIAM   The admission of his perjury.
FITZ-OSBERN   He will
   Deny it.
WILLIAM   And be damned.
FITZ-OSBERN   That won't secure
   The throne.
WILLIAM   Well, art thou man or midwife?
   Deliver.
FITZ-OSBERN   The Count of Burgundy –
WILLIAM   A traitor.
FITZ-OSBERN   Because you vanquished him. That war set half
   Your realm against you – nor had you won at all
   Save that you trusted in your friends.
WILLIAM   And promised
   Them reward.
FITZ-OSBERN   Yes, of course, but had you not
   Tilted them at Burgundy with combined
   Appeals of pelf and fealty, they had charged
   At your quintain,* either then or after.
WILLIAM   My power now is indubítable.
FITZ-OSBERN   Your power is your reputation,
   The which this trembling controverts.
WILLIAM   You witnessed with what ease I did subdue
   The Bretons.
FITZ-OSBERN   The Bretons are not English,
   Nor did you brave the sea.
WILLIAM   Now – there's
   The enterprise. Keep on, sir, or are all
   Thy postholes* dug? Let the sea fill 'em in
   Again.
FITZ-OSBERN   It can be done.
      Pause

---

quintain object mounted on a post and used as a target in jousting practice
posthole hole for securing wooden posts used in the framing of a simple medieval dwelling

WILLIAM   An if* it could –
   Yet – even could I tempt away
   These friends from the margins of their fealty
   To ships and foreign war, citing every
   Gross enticement that might stead the main
   And parch the gunnels of their dread – still,
   With even men enough and horses, spears,
   Shields, sails, ships to ferry all
   Unfoundering across, your panoply's
   Fantastic, can only loom like limnèd vapor
   In the offing. For rightful kings, of proper
   Lineage and descent, though surely troubled by
   This kite's scavenged majesty, will –
   In keeping with their cultish niceties –
   Doubtless view him the justly chosen,
   And term my challenge the renouncement!
FITZ-OSBERN   A deputation will be sent to every
   Monarch within the reach of Normandy,
   To report this earl's sacrilegious lies.
   Such betrayals of oath, homage, and betrothal –
   Featly couched and oiled – cannot fail
   In the offense of royals who've been more
   Honorably anointed.
WILLIAM   That may be so,
   But even in offense they'll not condone
   A deposition, lest their own crowns seem
   To fit too snugly.
FITZ-OSBERN   The papacy might bless
   Your action.
WILLIAM   The world has 'mights' enough. Speak
   Thy looks, man! You'd unsack Croesus'* hoard
   By the coin!
FITZ-OSBERN On my way hither, I

An if (archaic) if; provided that
Croesus ancient king of Lydia renowned for his great wealth

Encountered the abbot Lanfranc coming down
　　　From your chapel.
WILLIAM　　　　　　From synod* with my wife.
　　　He must have all the news.
FITZ-OSBERN　　　　　　He did seem to.
WILLIAM　And what said he to you?
FITZ-OSBERN　　　　　　　　That Cardinal Hildebrand
　　　In Rome – a former pupil in his priory
　　　Who holds great influence o'er the pontiff –
　　　Might convince the pope to sanctify
　　　This enterprise.
WILLIAM　　　　And so one poison cures
　　　Another – does this one have a serum?! Still –
　　　What must I pawn?
FITZ-OSBERN　　　　The abbot said it should
　　　Appear – and there he placed the emphasis –
　　　Appear that you concede in judgment of
　　　The matter to the pope.
WILLIAM　　　　　So we truckle
　　　To a churchman, then?! What were his arguments?
FITZ-OSBERN　My lord?
WILLIAM　　　　　　Reasons – grounds for his surmise?!
FITZ-OSBERN　He did not give them.
WILLIAM　　　　　　　　　Stays he at the cloisters?
FITZ-OSBERN　Yes, but I know not how long.
WILLIAM　　　　　　　　　　　Send someone
　　　To retrieve him there. No – I'll send my wife –
　　　She's his arch familiar.
FITZ-OSBERN　Lanfranc's a subtle man and guileful,
　　　But he has served your ends before –
　　　Many times – and oft to most striking effect –
　　　Proving the usefulness of his agency.
　　　He would not fail in this proposèd venture.

synod　church council convened to discuss ecclesiastical affairs

WILLIAM I won't be ruled from Rome, nor manipulated
   By a monk. This time he'll play out the part
   He's given. Enough. The thing proceeds.
   Those deputations we spoke of – they must
   Be coached to courtesies, not proclamations.
   When the abbot succeeds – and I do not doubt
   He will – then shall we butter and baste
   The royal dudgeons of our brethren
   With a pontiff's ampulla.* Now go, sir,
   And call our war council together –
   Summon Roger de Beaumont, Bishop Odo,
   The Count of Mortain, William Warrenne,
   And whomsoever else thou judgest fit
   To plan invasion.
FITZ-OSBERN   I shall, my lord.
   Exit FITZ-OSBERN
WILLIAM Guy de Burgundy – thou wast a traitor –
   But of a regal line.
   This slave'd fright buzzards for a taste
   Of royalty. Have at it hyena – laugh
   Thy throat's worth – I'll spill it out.
   Exit

Act II scene 5: England. The coast of Northumbria.

Sounds of battle, then several men retreat across the stage, HIRELING 1 & 2 following

HIRELING 2 They're pulling the longships off! Make haste!
HIRELING 1 Is that our fleet?! I won't stay with him longer –
   he knew of this ambush and yet drove us into it.
HIRELING 2 He can't a' known – we'd a' landed somewhere else.

---

ampulla glass vial containing anointing oil used by clergy during certain rites and ceremonies

HIRELING 1   I don't believe it – we sailed without a lookout on his knarr,* threatening any safety, and he was oddly humored: yesternight, when the hairy star* 'gan flaring, he mocked and made as if he'd shoot it with an arrow, then, before the fogs came 'n it was brighter, he said it omened nothing and bade the helmsman steer by it.
HIRELING 2   What can it mean? Do you think it be an evil star?
HIRELING 1   It don't portend good. I think the heavens mean to scourge his life.
HIRELING 2   But we've sworn to death on bibles – or the covers anyway – th't we'd be his men and follow 'im.
HIRELING 1   Not to a fool's exit.
HIRELING 2   Should we kill 'im then? I've often thought on it.
   Exeunt

Act II scene 6: The same.

Enter EDWIN and THEGN from opposite sides

THEGN   My lord, the battle's over with scarcely a man lost on our side. Most of his band yielded before the fray – of the rest, they're either fled with him or groan-gone – scattered in the brackish mud.
EDWIN   Godwinson – is he clay again?
THEGN   He never left the shore, sire, for us to cut him down, and though we launched a palisade at him – when once you made his figure known – not a spear or arrow hit the mark.
EDWIN   So he's escaped?
THEGN   He is, my lord, with some one or two hundred of his men, in knarrer and several longships.
EDWIN   Bring to me those prisoners we spoke of.

knarr   merchant ship of the period
hairy star   aka Halley's Comet, which appeared in March of 1066

Exit THEGN
Escaped. Again thou dost delay thy doom
With a feckless serendipity.
Canst e'er obey a writ or ban
Not endited* by thy vagaries?!
Pause
Licentious cur,
Thou canst not flee me far enough.
Die – suffer and die – batter thy brains
In thy headlong wildness.
Enter MORCAR
MORCAR Edwin, we've driven them from the kingdom –
All but a remnant have surrendered!
EDWIN But in that remnant lay our proof of triumph.
MORCAR I saw that Tostig lived – I cast at him
In a volley – my housecarls and fyrdsmen
Cheered in the attempt.
EDWIN You should have stayed
By me. Your brashness is disgusting.
MORCAR I am sorry, brother.
EDWIN Do not mix in
The ranks again. Brother, we must espouse
Each other's fortunes and keep them vital against
The rest, whose baser nature's wallow in foul
Hypocrisies.
MORCAR I will be more vigilant.
EDWIN Morcar, only in our joint and pure
Prosperity resides continuance.
MORCAR You forget our sister.
EDWIN *(aside)* The ready mare.* *(Aloud)* No –
She'll couple with our royal sire. We two
Will nephew kings, *(Aside)* if we cannot kill their kin.

endite [1] put in writing [2] (obsolete) dictate; prescribe
ready mare female horse exhibiting signs of heat

Reenter THEGN with soldiers escorting HIRELING 1 & 2 as prisoners

THEGN   Here are the prisoners. *(To MORCAR)* How did your first fight favor you, my lord? Quite a thrashing!

MORCAR   Well, sir, well, though the…banished lord survived, sir.

THEGN   He did, sire, but I hope there won't be mutton* for that.

EDWIN   *(to HIRELINGS)* You men served Tostig Godwinson.

HIRELING 1   Aye, sir.

HIRELING 2   Not I, sir – or, I mean – not me, sir.

EDWIN *(to HIRELING 2)* I've seen you close about his company.

HIRELING 2   I have a twin, sir.

HIRELING 1   Imbecile, this is the Earl of Mercia.

HIRELING 2   No twin – not one – I look just like meself, sir's what I meant – uh – I thought you was someone else – a' old friend.

EDWIN   I don't keep them that long. *(To HIRELING 1)* Why did he stay so close by his ship?

HIRELING 1   I do not know, sire, but that perhaps the fatal star made him suspicious.

EDWIN   Was he forewarned in any way directly?

HIRELING 1   It could be so – but he had acted strangely for some weeks before.

EDWIN   Strangely how?

HIRELING 1   Like as he'd destroy himself – though it sometimes seemed pretended.

EDWIN *(aside to THEGN)* Drown them in the surf. Let them float there.

MORCAR *(overhearing)* But they did voluntarily surrender.

EDWIN   That makes them no less guilty.

THEGN *(to MORCAR)*   They murdered
   Many nobles in your earldom, sire.

MORCAR   So make them bondsmen then.

---

mutton   that is, typical fare rather than something tastier which might reasonably be expected at a victory feast

EDWIN *(to MORCAR)* What is this weakness – this compassion?
 Lance it off – they cannot see it. Act with
 Unfettered calculation or you'll die bound,
 Ignobly, like these men here – or,
 Being as you are so…comradely –
 Upon the spear-points o' those friends
 You'd laugh with on the line.
  He motions to THEGN, who exits with soldiers escorting HIRELINGS
MORCAR Is every man but you malevolent?
  Exit MORCAR

Act II scene 7: A ship off the coast of Northumbria.

 TOSTIG stands astern

TOSTIG The sea too is all inanimate,
 Though it float us o'er like dreams to our auroras –
 Just so much excrescent scurf and foam,
 Lifeless as these wrecks of men whose empty,
 Splintered hulls bestrew the shore. This whole
 Sodden waste of world's a shattered cenotaph.
  Pause
 And yet, I might thus linger for a time,
 But the drabness and oppressive squalor
 Of it all pollutes and soils me…like
 The smeared rag a wench'd use to scrub
 The dirt around. Mine's her dung-daubed hovel,
 Maggots squirming in the rushes.* Or
 Perhaps it's all just fixtured in my brain,
 And I blow a grimy gather* to make the world

---

rushes thick marsh grasses commonly thrown over earthen floors of the time to scent the air and act as an absorbent – they were much less commonly replaced
gather (glassmaking) blob of molten glass at the end of a blowpipe

Opaque. Enough. What boots this taffrailing* –
What grandiose pronouncements –
Plucking down the comet star? We are all
Hapless engines of our own reflection –
Looking out we only see into ourselves,
And even then but partway to the pith.
   Pause
Harold, where's thy kingly countervail?
Set out the wine and all thy arguments –
Both'll be drained ere thou retirest
To wallow in the dregs. Yea, to bed with ye,
Apostle, too good a man for such feeble believing.
Is't not a cowardice? – But to believe –
To find oneself in the lees of it?
There must be some sensible shame in that –
There certainly seemeth ease.
   Pause
The sea gluts and sickens me – my thoughts
Writhe like slimy eels inside my brain.
   Pause
Will I live to see you stagger off again,
Brother – to waver like a reed when 't last
You raise yourself to sermonize your dogs
Before the fire, before your leaving –
Aye, before leaving only such night left
For us to make eterne!
It will not do. All the peace wherewith
I might be soothed or tamed is spent –
Or spoke into a grubby hole and covered o'er.*
Besmirched I am in bloody dirt and brine,

---

taffrailing portmanteau suggested by the deprecatory verb "rail." A taffrail is a rail extending across the stern of some ships.
Or spoke...o'er (Greek mythology) an allusion to the legendary King Midas, who was punished with ass's ears by Apollo for judging Pan the winner of a musical contest between the two gods. Midas was able to conceal the ears under a Phrygian cap but the servant who cut his hair knew about them and, unable to keep such a secret, dug a hole and whispered into it, "King Midas has ass's ears."

And though I'm not stained through but few scraps
Still show white – I cannot think they'll stay so.

Act II scene 8: London. The king's great hall on Thorney Island.

HAROLD, EDWIN, MORCAR, and ROBERT *consult a large map. Several* HERALDS *stand by at attention, evidently awaiting orders. A messenger enters and gives* HAROLD *a letter, which he then briefly reads.*

HAROLD *(destroying letter)* Thus ends our stormy correspondence,
   William – and though I never met thy daughter,
   I fear thy pertinacity must be in her,
   Which is quite enough to warn me off.
   (To messenger) Return this message to your importuning duke:
   England will not have him or his daughter.
   And, rather than threat the skies with this
   Bootless thundering, if he's to send us
   Real tempests, well, then we'll put
   Our oilskins* on.
     Exit messenger
   No, it must be the Isle of Wight –
   We'll catch the wind that way to where'er they land,
   And ram their boats up on the shore.
EDWIN   How if they bypass Dover? You'd squander the fleet.
   The northern fyrd should be advanced to Essex
   To guard the coast there – a contingent could
   Be left in York.
HAROLD   Robert, what do you think?

---

oilskin heavy cloth garment waterproofed with oil

ROBERT   That London would be vulnerable, sire.
   Yet, though I am no war planner,
   I know what 'tis to risk, and I knew the young
   Duke: he'd poach his deer by bow and stable.*
HAROLD   Indeed, the man would not parlay his chance,
   He'd purchase double sureties. Mercia,
   Morcar, keep your forces near the Humber.
   Enter CLERK with dispatches
CLERK   *(handing dispatches to HAROLD)* Your majesty.
HAROLD   *(to EDWIN)* This is not news from Flanders. King
   Malcolm*
   Won't abide him,* but there are those who might.
   (To HERALDS, handing each dispatches) Before the full shire
   courts, you understand –
   With every ealdorman, reeve, and bishop present
   Who'd sit to hear a hundred's indetermined suit.*
   These seals'll wrest their promptitude.
   We cannot fail here men – not at the start –
   This muster begins with you, and your loyalties'
   Sufferance. Art thou English?!
HERALDS   Aye, my lord – Aye – Yes, your majesty – Aye.
HAROLD   Then ride!
   Exeunt HERALDS
         Clerk, where is the exchequer?
   Be sure he's sent for. And where are those mandates
   For the Lord of Clavering?
ROBERT   Your majesty.
HAROLD   I will inure you to it.* Morcar – does he
   Not look the lord?

bow and stable   method of hunting which posed the least danger to the hunters, it entailed hounds driving the quarry – often an entire herd – to a predetermined place where archers stood ready in ambush
King Malcolm   the King of Scotland
him   Tostig
shire courts…indetermined suit   each Anglo-Saxon shire was divided into smaller administrative units called hundreds (cf. note on **wapentake**, pg 4). Any legal matter incapable of resolution by a local hundred court would be referred up to the shire.
I will inure you to it   apparently Harold has conferred upon Robert manorial land and a title

MORCAR   Most heartily, your highness.
HAROLD   You stand too tall in the saddle, sir, to be
    Unpropertied.
ROBERT   I should slouch in it now
    Without the steward's grooming.
HAROLD *(to CLERK)*   Please sir,
    The mandates. Do we need more scribes?!
CLERK   The exchequer
    Is assisting them, your majesty.
HAROLD   Ah –
    Forgive me – I've been whirling about since morning
    Like a swarm whose hive the wind knocked down.
    Bring the mandates when they're ready.
        Exit CLERK
    So, then –
MORCAR   The south, sire?
HAROLD   Yes – the south.
    The call-up* runs from Kent to Dorset. When
    The couriers have delivered and our orders
    Are fulfilled, I'll lead my housecarls down
    To join the southern fyrd in Chichester.
    Clavering – that hath a pleasant ring –
    Clavering will unite the Cinque Port fleets*
    From Sandwich to Hastings, and conduct them to
    The Sussex rendezvous –
EDWIN   For transport to
    An island? But if the duke's armies land before
    A wind that's contrary –
HAROLD   As yours is,
    So constantly? – Then we'll surely be marooned…–
    Then we row to shore, man,
    And dash the fords to greet him!

call-up order to report for military service
Cinque Port fleets a loose confederation of (originally five) seaport towns along the southeastern coast of England, which furnished ships for the king's service in return for certain privileges and limited autonomy

Edwin, Tostig is not vanquished – you must
Think more of the north's defense.
EDWIN   Defense from York?! –
It's just as well – he'd lay waste your earldom
Ere I could meet him in the field.
HAROLD   Is that so –
Then it's well we speak in hypotheticals.
   Reenter CLERK with mandates
(To CLERK) Oh, welcome, sir – welcome – take my hand!
You look excellent well, sir. *(Aside to CLERK)* Can you forge
me a proscription?! *(Aloud)* Better even than when last we
met. How fare the children?! Wife? Priest? *(Aside to CLERK)*
Tavern keeper? *(Takes mandates from CLERK. Aloud.)* Oh,
you are too kind sir, really. *(Aside to CLERK)* Nod, I beseech
you. *(CLERK nods. Aloud.)* Thank you, sir – most gracious –
thank you.
CLERK *(still nodding)* Yes, your majesty.
HAROLD *(aside to CLERK)* The exchequer?
CLERK *(aside to HAROLD)* – Will be along directly, your majesty.
HAROLD *(aside to CLERK)* Very well then.
   Exit CLERK. Enter EDITH unnoticed.
What a charming man, Robert, and to think,
Only 'sir' for a title – and even that
Superfluous. Do I corrupt you, Clavering?
ROBERT   Corrupt, sire? An if I know this word,
'Corrupt,' it's not a title does it, but
The tethering.*
HAROLD *(handing him mandates)* Even the mewed up* falcon
Swoops beneath the hood.*

---

tethering (falconry) securing a bird with a tether, usu. by means of the jesses (see note on pg 33), prevents it from unexpectedly flying at prey when being carried on the fist or moving from a perch during training
mewed up (falconry) raptors are housed in an enclosure called a "mews"
hood (falconry) to calm a bird esp. during the early stages of its training, whether perched on the fist or in its mews, its face and eyes are often covered with a closely fitted hood (cf. note on **unseel**, pg 51)

ROBERT   Indeed, sire,
  Manned but never tamed.*
  He starts to leave
EDITH *(to ROBERT)* Godspeed, Robert Fitz-Wimark.
ROBERT *(to EDITH)* Dost thou address the Lord of Clavering?
EDITH   What – airs already, sir?
ROBERT   Hah!
  No, milady – or only one – in which
  It seems I must fly creanced at the pitch.*
EDITH   Speak out if so, but stay on,
  And serve in your own best capacity.
  Don't mistake him Robert – the king only
  Wants to please you.
ROBERT   The king please me?!
  Then whom shall I?
EDITH   Well, there are many
  Gentle young –
ROBERT   Madam, thy womanish banter
  Doth but detain me from more lordlier commissions.
EDITH   Goodbye, sir.
ROBERT   I shall reflect on your wisdom.
  Smiles to your ladyship – and keen hounds!
  Farewell!
  Exit ROBERT
MORCAR   But once the ships've been descried,
  Can the scouts post with sufficient speed?
EDWIN   Not if he lands too distantly – driftwood
  Might be faster.
HAROLD   The coast guards only need
  Ignite their beacons – when the signal line reaches

Manned but never tamed (falconry) a bird is said to be "manned" when fully accustomed to a falconer's presence, however, raptors are not truly domesticable

creanced at the pitch (falconry) i.e. tethered while soaring. A "creance" is a long training cord used before a bird can be trusted to fly free; "pitch" is the height which, having achieved, a raptor will maintain before stooping at prey or a lure.

    Wight, we launch, and fan past the fires
    To the duke's encampment.
EDWIN *(seeing EDITH)* You find my disputatiousness of-
    fends.
    My interests, it may be, are not
    Altogether yours – but in this both
    Must comport: thy dane-wife's* presence here
    Flouts all Christian modesty. It defiles
    My sister's bridebed.
MORCAR   Peace, brother – the king
    Meant no offense.
EDWIN   What is this? Are you
   Siblinged to me? Thou art a lackey to
   The king.
MORCAR   I am your brother, Edwin.
EDWIN   I see
   No brother here, save one whose own'd murder you!
MORCAR   How can I please you?! What can I do?!
EDITH *(turning to go)* I should not have come here.
HAROLD   Stay where you are, Edith.
EDWIN   Did my realm dues not exceed the cost
    Of a requiting act, I should knock
    This woman down. Your majesty, I take my leave.
      Exit EDWIN
HAROLD   Placate your brother, Morcar – assure him
    No provocation was intended – that
    My course remains unchanged: to marry
    Your sister o' Sunday.
MORCAR   Yes, your majesty.
HAROLD   His gloominess'd encave the sky – you must
    Recall him from it.
MORCAR   My lord, I will try, but...
    Something is amiss in him.

dane-wife common-law wife; longtime mistress

HAROLD   Perhaps he thinks that I misprize his counsel,
   Or would shun him from his own renown.
   For your honors both and my alliance with them,
   Say the king himself will come tomorrow
   To bear you hither.
MORCAR   Yes, your majesty.
   Exit MORCAR. Enter EXCHEQUER with account books, pen, and ink.
HAROLD *(to EXCHEQUER)* I will be with you presently.
   EXCHEQUER retires
   (To EDITH) What a performance! But I sent for you
   Too soon – we had not yet concluded.
EDITH   You
   Are certain of invasion then?
HAROLD   Of an intent,
   Edith, yes – spies confirm so.
   The duke has ordered the construction of a fleet.
EDITH   But has he men enough to challenge you?
HAROLD   Not in Normandy – and his recruitment
   Elsewhere laggers.
EDITH   Would Tostig join him?
HAROLD   Never as a mercenary, and William
   Doesn't seek for partners.
EDITH   Are you afraid?
HAROLD   No more than were I in a battle now.
EDITH   Is that where now you find yourself?
   Pause
HAROLD   You cannot stay here, Edith.
EDITH   I know. Why was I ever brought?
   Did you think that simply being king
   You'd change men's minds? That's why wars are fought:
   Because two men do not agree.
HAROLD   You knew this was like to happen – I could not rule,
   Much less levy our defense, without
   The Church's backing.

EDITH   Or the earl's.
HAROLD   Or the earl's – or my overlord
   In heaven. This marriage is expedient –
   No woman, from slave to queen, ever bore
   Thy beauty nor enchanted with thy mystery.
   But king – it consumes me, Edith – the whole of it –
   Lours o'er my more private nature,
   Confining me to fish ponds when I would lose
   Me in a wilderness –
   Banning all mortal, mere self-regardings
   Like whores from a novitiate.*
   Perhaps I overstate. But I must do
   This right – or these – there is so much to be done.
EDITH   And you mean to do it all alone.
HAROLD   I do not mean to – it isn't so
   Deliberate as that. It is God's choosing.
EDITH   For our sake, Harold, make it also your own.
HAROLD   You are right, Edith – and my own.
   I shall visit you in Bosham sometimes,
   If you will have me.
EDITH   I do not know
   If I shall stay there.
HAROLD   Will you if I keep
   Away?
EDITH   I cannot say.
HAROLD   Surely you'll make at least a brief return.
   Join me on my way to the Isle of Wight –
   We'll ride home from the road one more time.
EDITH   I should go, sire – a gentleman awaits you.
HAROLD   Goodbye, Edith. Come, sir, I've kept
   You too long – we've a treasury to expend.
EDITH   Goodbye.

novitiate   prospective member of a religious order, usu. quite young, who has not yet taken vows

Exit EDITH. EXCHEQUER comes forward and hands HAROLD some books. Pause.

EXCHEQUER   She's gone, your majesty. Sire?

HAROLD   You have the Wessex incomes?

EXCHEQUER   They are before you, your majesty.

HAROLD   *(looking at books)* Ah, yes. So then – and East Anglia – good – we'll weigh the rest tomorrow. *(Pause)* To begin: in county Kent – of thegns holding directly or by median, to include churls and freeholders and lesser yeoman of consequence…

Act II scene 9: Norway. The longhouse of Eystein Orre.

HARDRADA, EYSTEIN, LEIF, ARNULF, GUNNAR, THIODULF, and FRIREK sit around a large table that ELSA is clearing after a meal. Many have been drinking.

HARDRADA   Let Hakon hide himself, bind a new sheathe
    For my heart-anger – the Dane king should
    Be dead – and Einar bought his own
    Blood death. Eystein Orre remembers
    Einar's wife, how she wailed at
    Her husband's gashes – how beautiful she was.
    Thiodulf: sing again that verse you made
    From what the Nid folk* said – of Thyra's
    Brain-sick anguish, her wasteful tears.

THIODULF   Einar's wife weeps as she sews
    His gambesons,* sobs pulling fish off
    The forge hooks – howling she clubs them
    For the cauldron pot with soft oiled hands.

Nid folk   i.e. people of Nidaros (modern Trondheim). Located on the western coast, Nidaros was at this time the capital of Norway and the country's most important city.
gambeson   padded garment worn beneath armor to dampen the effect of blunt blows

HARDRADA No woman makes a worthy widow –
　He looks at EYSTEIN
　Nor man a mourner – long. Hist, Hearthmen,*
　Who'd devise a lighter lay – something
　Lusty for the loins?
ARNULF Noble Eystein – with thy consent,
　Host-friend, I'll improvise a song upon
　Thy servant girl.
EYSTEIN　　　　　Sing – she is called Elsa.
ARNULF Elsa's bodice – stained from leaning
　At our feast – from brushing the beef tray
　That steamed with meat. Katren too would steam
　If she knew what Arnulf dreams.
　Mild acclamation
HARDRADA　　　　　　　　Deft – but tamed
　By the tail of it.
GUNNAR　　　Or tucked 'tween 's legs.
EYSTEIN *(to ARNULF)* Arnulf, she hath been tupped before.
　Take her,
　If she will go.
GUNNAR　　　Or shall we send for thy Hel-wife?!*
ARNULF Bitter is thy battle-making, Gunnar.
EYSTEIN Take her.
　Exit ARNULF with ELSA
LEIF　　　　　　War King, unlock thy word-craft –
　Honor thy hearth mates with a verse on the theme.
HARDRADA Then, may my art seduce the air
　And stir thine ear shells with a wave journey:
　A fiery slave from Sicily I took
　Across to Africa. She padded the planks
　Naked, shameless – we shook the aft castle.

Hearthmen literally, men privileged to share the king's hearth; these handpicked and usu. high-born Norse nobles, having earned the king's favor through loyalty and acts of courage, formed the inner circle of his most trusted companions

Hel-wife (Norse mythology) Hel is the goddess of the underworld, unpleasant both in disposition and appearance

Then she sprang to shore, spurned my smiles –
Earned an axe-kiss for not yielding.
Acclamation
EYSTEIN   A masterly performance.
THIODULF   Very skillful, indeed.
GUNNAR   Stubborn slave so to resist you, a king.
  She did deserve her ending.
HARDRADA   She should not
  Have resisted, then no blood had spilled –
  My purse had puffed with her slave price –
  But she could not ken the danger goading
  Her mulishness – thought vain struggles would fend off fate.
  She was wrong.
EYSTEIN   There is no proof* 'gainst dying, nor force
  To fight the Wyrd.*
HARDRADA   Eystein Orre, what
  You say is true enough, and must be so,
  With no defying – the Christ knows this
  And teaches us – so did Woden Lord*
  Before. But braveness endures – the spear-din
  Deafens your wordplay – finds life
  A flesh-hold in the clangor.
EYSTEIN   I too
  Find life there, Folk King, and pray
  For Hildr's* coming on – but…hearts hold
  Other longings.
HARDRADA   Let us cease this thought-trade
  Noble friend – it's time thy verse was sung.
SEVERAL AT ONCE   Frirek! Frirek first!

proof (archaic) proven power of resistance
Wyrd corresponding roughly to the eastern concept of "karma" – though without a commensurate moral dimension – Wyrd refers to a process beyond human control in which past actions work through time to shape the present. Although Wyrd can be personal in nature, it is often linked with families, tribes, and even entire races.
Woden Lord (Norse mythology) variant of "Odin," the chief Norse god
Hildr (Norse mythology) one of the Valkyries, winged and armored female goddesses who conduct the souls of the bravest warriors slain in battle to privileged afterlives among the gods

GUNNAR We must hear Frirek.
EYSTEIN Frirek? *(To FRIREK)* Berserkman,* wouldst thou sing?
FRIREK I will.
EYSTEIN Of war women?
FRIREK No.
EYSTEIN We long for thy verse.
FRIREK Gytha is Leif's lass – lovely as a valley,
And...very lovely, the cleft between her tits.
I wish just once she'd fuck me, even
After Leif.
  Laughter and acclamation
EYSTEIN   Straight from the World Mill.*
LEIF She won't have thee, Frirek, as well ye wot!
Ring Giver, bind this Fenrir* –
He glares like the gray wolf at her father's home.
HARDRADA Frirek – thou hast lain insatiably
With a full-most of our hearth maids.
Let Gytha wed this man ungorged with thy glut.
And Leif Andreasson, haste this lass
To a stavekirk,* for many men do thirst
For her, though they know the heat between you.
  Enter TOSTIG
THIODULF *(aside to HARDRADA)* The English, War King.
HARDRADA *(aside to THIODULF)*   Strangely
  haggard
In his eye-looks.
EYSTEIN   Frirek – the mead horn.

Berserkman variant of "berserker," both deriving from "bearsark" meaning "bear-shirted" in Old Norse – berserkers were known to wear the skins of wolves and bears into battle in order to terrify their enemies and, presumably, in the belief that they could thereby channel the spirits of the animals
World Mill (Norse mythology) according to tradition, the body of the primitive clay-giant Ymer, first inhabitant of the universe, was ground up in the great world-mill of the gods to form the earth
Fenrir (Norse mythology) monstrous wolf bound after much effort with a magic cord so as to prevent the fulfillment of several prophecies indicating that it would cause the gods great trouble
stavekirk Nordic wooden church of the time framed with vertically fitted planks and often featuring multiple gables with steeply pitched roofs

FRIREK He should drink ale.
EYSTEIN   Then you should fetch some.
   *FRIREK hands EYSTEIN the horn. EYSTEIN then passes it
   to TOSTIG, who drinks.*
GUNNAR A Westman comes – wanly seeks
   Bold Norway –
EYSTEIN Forbear, *(Aside to GUNNAR)* until his leaving.
TOSTIG   Or do not –
   Let me hear thy verse. *(GUNNAR is silent)* Shall I finish it?:
   A Westman comes – wanly seeks
   Bold Norway – wearily swallows
   A wretched mead – grieves th't life won't flee
   After such foulness.
      Murmurs
   Eystein, your bed box* sways.
EYSTEIN   You've been too long
   On the salt trails. Tostig Godwinson –
   West Lord, brother of the English king –
   Behold Harald Sigurdsson – yclept* Hardrada –
   Him of the hard counsel* – the King of Norway.
HARDRADA I have heard of your king's passing, that his crown
   Befell an earl. Why did he bid you here,
   Giftless, to our realm?
TOSTIG   I come unbidden
   Because I, too, have been disdained by England.
   My lands have been seized, my title snatched away –
   Pinned to a stripling. I come to whet
   Thy pride-slights and dread indignancies,
   To appeal of thine umbrage an army, battle-strong,
   A Norse horde to ransack Northumbria
   And win back my dominions.
      Pause

bed box in Scandinavian longhouses beds were often built into compact closets along the central living space; they might be curtained for a measure of privacy
yclept (archaic) called; known as
hard counsel a rough translation of the moniker "Hardrada"

HARDRADA   Long have
  The drakkar* lain lulled in Nidaros,
  Languished ungilt while their shield-scales parch on walls –
  Long have the hall thegns hungered for war,
  To settle their rage in a meeting of mail coats.
  But not for foreign war chiefs will
  The Northmen fight – not for English word-fame.
TOSTIG Is it true what they say in my homeland –
  That King Magnus your cousin sent envoys
  To Edward, proclaiming his right to the English
  Throne as well as Denmark's, devolved
  Through Hardacanute?
HARDRADA   How came he not
  To the heritage if he had such a right?
TOSTIG   Is Denmark
  Thine as it was thy predecessor's?
LEIF   He mocks you,
  King, but the Danes have naught to brag of:
  Many a vill there's flamed from our torch fires –
  Many a gift hall's* burned to the floor.
TOSTIG *(ignoring LEIF)* Canst not reply? Then I will tell thee:
  Magnus took Denmark 'cause he had the war chiefs
  On his side – you have not because they've been
  Against you. For the same reason, over time,
  King Magnus glozed his claim to England –
  He knew that nation wanted only Edward
  For its sovereign. Take England now –
  I can promise you that most of the principal lords will be our
  friends and help you, for nothing prevents me from being
  my brother's equal except a crown. All men know there's
  never been a greater warrior than you in the Northlands.

---

drakkar (Old Norse for "dragon ship," taken here and elsewhere as plural) Viking longship with a distinctive curved prow often carved into the shape of a dragon
gift hall aka mead hall, a large communal building where a lord or chieftain and his warriors gathered usu. for feasting or religious ceremonies

For fifteen years you've fought in Denmark
To tame an anfractuous thistle –
It would seem strange now to persist there
When all England could be trained to your form.
HARDRADA   Thy words are spear-sharp and pierce to my
Resolve, but must be closely pondered.
Eystein Orre – what is thy advisement?
EYSTEIN   His words, indeed, are strongly sensed, and sway
One toward the venture. Who would not sail
Again for glory-gold?
FRIREK   Give me both!
EYSTEIN *(aside to HARDRADA)* Yet...he hath but few men
and much
Ill repute. Promise always thrives
On the horizons – and Hakon's still alive –
The Danes could strike in our absence.
HARDRADA *(aside to EYSTEIN)*   Say
Thou wouldst not fight.
EYSTEIN *(aside to HARDRADA)* Only when Earth sinks
In Ocean.*
HARDRADA   West Lord – tomorrow we'll engage
Again, when thou art better rested. Now rise,
Hall friends, and make for the Thing-place,*
Where custom beckons we debate.
  Exeunt all but TOSTIG and EYSTEIN. EYSTEIN provides him
  with food.
GUNNAR *(offstage)* Oh, Katren – Arnulf? – No – Frirek, hast
thou seen Arnulf?
EYSTEIN   Go on, eat – thou hast had bread before.
  ARNULF, hurriedly dressing, crosses the stage
ARNULF *(exiting)* Katren?

Earth sinks in Ocean   (Norse mythology) disaster concluding the events of "Ragnarok,"
a series of calamities that will one day engulf both gods and men
Thing-place   designated outdoor meeting place where Scandinavian assemblies ("things")
of the people were convened to make laws, resolve disputes, elect officials etc.

Exit ARNULF. Laughter offstage.
TOSTIG   None I could not recognize.
EYSTEIN   Then close
   Thine eyes *(Aside)* as Orre doth.
      Exit EYSTEIN
TOSTIG   They are too open.
      He starts to eat
   But it's done. 'Less I find him i' the field –
   This bitterness our ending.
      Pause
   What matter is't mates meaning
   To endeavor – enfolds us all in one
   Design that should be infinite, or none?
   Or say not folds: ensnares.
   Stuck we are like flies in webs of ether,
   All along just waiting for the spider.
      Enter ELSA, somewhat unkempt
ELSA   Saw'st 'ou a spider? *(Looking)* Hath it hid?
TOSTIG   Check thy smock.
ELSA   If thou wilt thy trousers.
TOSTIG   Where's the ale?
ELSA   In a cask.
TOSTIG   Get me some.
ELSA   I won't serve a lout.
TOSTIG   Nor should ye, though thou art a hussy.
ELSA   Dost 'ou hate all the lasses, or just them
   That acts too free?
TOSTIG   Them's the ones I like.
      Pause
ELSA   The cask's i' the corner.
      Exit ELSA
TOSTIG *(getting ale)*   Tostig Godwinson,
   West lout. Thou art fool to thyself.

Act II scene 10: Normandy. The duke's castle in Rouen.

ODO and a large group of noblemen quietly converse. A SERVANT attends them. LANFRANC's presence goes unnoticed. Upon FITZ-OSBERN's entrance ODO approaches him and the two draw apart from the rest of the group.

FITZ-OSBERN   He is on the stairs.
ODO   King Philip?*
FITZ-OSBERN   He did not say.
ODO   Count Conan's dead.
FITZ-OSBERN   Yes – his horn was tipped with toxin.
ODO   Was it done by you?
FITZ-OSBERN   No, but it was needful, and 'twill keep Brittany in strife.
ODO   They're cowards besides – yet the need's such we might conscript thieves.
FITZ-OSBERN   The King of France will lend us troops.
ODO   We must have more – the summer's wasting.
FITZ-OSBERN   And Count Eustace – he hath pledged us fifty ships.
ODO   Fifty – that might appease the rocks. What of Aquitane – the second embassy? Has Poland sent answer?
FITZ-OSBERN   No – still nothing. You would know 'fore I.
ODO   Lillebonne* is long past now.
FITZ-OSBERN   Wouldst thou now prefer the opposition?
ODO   Not and so express to you.
FITZ-OSBERN   Indeed, nor me neither.
   Enter WILLIAM
WILLIAM *(to SERVANT)* Where is the duchess?
SERVANT   Walking the grounds, I do believe, your grace.
WILLIAM   Is she alone?

King Philip   the King of France, to whom William has just paid a visit
Lillebonne   council of the Norman baronage called by Duke William earlier in the year, ostensibly to discuss the prospective invasion but in actuality to exact pledges of military support

SERVANT The children are with her. Shall I say you are here?
   Pause
WILLIAM No – do not.
   (To FITZ-OSBERN and ODO) For the promise of some future force
   The king has trothed an army to our use.
FITZ-OSBERN Welcome news, sire.
WILLIAM Yes.
FITZ-OSBERN Bishop?
ODO My lord, welcome, but also quite expected. Harold will still have twice our number.
WILLIAM Then we'll be half the fewer – what of it?
ODO Nothing in battle, to be sure, but we may lack those needed for peace.
WILLIAM Bishop Odo – keep thy miter coifed* –
   Thou art not here for peace.
ODO Then I cannot promise victory.
WILLIAM What wouldst then, swear on our defeat?!
FITZ-OSBERN We shall have more men.
ODO *(ignoring WILLIAM)* Let us hope. When the blasphemer's dead more'll come.
FITZ-OSBERN Yes – certainly.
ODO But what sort – I doubt of their quality.
WILLIAM Are the ships yet constructed?
ODO Nearly all are complete.
WILLIAM The sails?
ODO They will be ready.
WILLIAM And shall we give up now?
ODO Give up, my lord?
FITZ-OSBERN *(aside to WILLIAM)* Paris to Rouen is a very long ride.
WILLIAM *(seeing LANFRANC)* It is, but not so long as from Rome. Lanfranc, what is thy success?

---

keep thy miter coifed a miter is a bishop's headdress; a coif is a close-fitting chainmail cap or hood – William admonishes the soldier/bishop to restrict his attention to straightforward military matters

LANFRANC *(coming forward)* I should be in terror if I displeased you, cunning duke.

WILLIAM Thou hast not yet. Now speak – and no slyness.

LANFRANC As you wish, great duke, but I beg you, do not censure me for humbly observing – from report – what seems to be, as yet, an insufficient force to shoulder this undertaking.

WILLIAM Hast thou ever spoke of aught firsthand,
Whether there or no?

LANFRANC *(resuming)* – And that – pardon my modesty – those lay enticements proffered – of bounty and titles and copious estates – seem not to have lured, thus far at least, a plentiful sum of men from beyond Normandy to follow you. I am a poor monk not schooled at all in these concernments but… would your ranks not rapidly increase if the Holy Father deemed you England's lawful claimant and the king there excommunicate?

ODO They would.

WILLIAM I know thee too well, monk – thou hast done it!

LANFRANC His Holiness bade me present to you this ring – its band contains a relic of St. Peter.

He gives WILLIAM ring

WILLIAM To what purpose?

LANFRANC Wearing, most dreaded duke – if you'll vouchsafe it – on the sacred mission his Holiness enjoins –

WILLIAM *(dryly)* Yes?

LANFRANC *(producing decree, sealed and tied with ribbon)* – Which is, in fine, to chastise the English perjurer and restore his church unto the Papal fold.

WILLIAM *(putting on ring)* Style it howsoe'er thou like'st.

LANFRANC And to hold the subject kingdom, savvy lord, as a fief to Rome.

Pause

WILLIAM Curled to the sting. Where doth thy service cringe
In this, abbot?

LANFRANC Why, my gracious duke, are our masters not the same?
WILLIAM Give me the parchment!
  LANFRANC hands decree to WILLIAM, who opens and looks at it briefly, then passes it to FITZ-OSBERN
  (To FITZ-OSBERN and ODO) Send out word to the monarchs –
  No knight will scan the justice but,
  A rich life or a swift flight to heaven –
  God and Mammon both:* they'll all seize
  On that.
LANFRANC *(overhearing)* Oh Duke, be not too wroth, but, misapprehending perhaps the extent of my authority there, I suffered His Holiness' decree to be ratified on your behalf, and – from a most solicitous regard for your preparations' urgency – relayed, as I departed Rome, to a great number of the kings in your petition.
WILLIAM Didst thou! Well – the pope may claim relief*
  But only I will rule in England.
FITZ-OSBERN *(reading decree)* Remarkable!
LANFRANC *(to FITZ-OSBERN)* Yes. *(To WILLIAM)* That difficult provision, honored duke, was debated most vociferously – a cardinal in attendance assured me of it – but Archdeacon Hildebrand, once my own gifted scholar and a far more subtle reasoner than I, defeated my objections –
WILLIAM Wilt thou ever slough the shame?!
  Church bells sound. LANFRANC is momentarily distracted.
  Yes, I hear them – finish.
LANFRANC *(resuming)* – And admonished me to inform your lordship – which I now do, with great trepidation – that, should you make use of the Holy Father's blessed decree, either for the aggrandizement of yourself or your armies – really, it seems, in any instrumental way – then you do so

God and Mammon both see Matthew 6:24
relief fee due from a vassal to a lord upon succeeding to an estate

at peril of latterly incurring, I'm beholden to say, some-
what more onerous obligations and or exactions.
WILLIAM   Is that so.
LANFRANC   Well, I must to vespers* as you know.
WILLIAM   Excellent – then thou art through,
And well bethought, all of thy remarks.
Now go on, leave, I dare not keep thee –
Only teach me first, learned monk,
If thou art able, just how it is, despite
The manifold advantages that redound
From thy offices, and the exceeding rareness
Of our interviews, I never in my life
Feel more relieved than when I'm quit o' thee!
   Short pause
LANFRANC   Surely it were prodigal instruction, humble duke,
to teach that which your lordship already knows.
WILLIAM   Fitz-Osbern, see him out!
   Exeunt FITZ-OSBERN with LANFRANC
ODO   The decree shall be staged at once in those kingdoms
he neglected.
WILLIAM   *(struggling to remove ring)* Bloody midget ring – what's
he, size these relics to himself?!
ODO   Many more men will join us now.
WILLIAM   Many more men, yes, and many more
Expectancies.

---

vespers evening prayers; sixth of the seven canonical hours, usu. in the late afternoon or early evening

Act II scene 11: Norway. Port of Nidaros on the western coast. A dock along the shore.

    Enter EYSTEIN and THIODULF

EYSTEIN   No, Thiodulf, thou hast the lyre –
   And the ready song.
THIODULF   Then so it goes:
   The dragons seethe and lash at the swells,
   Spew spray to the fjord tops –
   Across wharf docks –
   Where frighted women watch,
   Clutch close the young children.
   Then comes the king –
   Beckons from shore –
   And now the ships are spellbound –
   Ten thousand oars sweep in unison,
   And the whole harbor
   Wings for the sea.
EYSTEIN   Still a bracing verse –
   But where is the king?
THIODULF   Stayed at the cathedral
   Shrine.
EYSTEIN   Saint Olaf honor his prayers –
THIODULF   And lead us,
   With the son of Jorn,* to triumph.
EYSTEIN   Yes.
   (raising flask) To triumph or a vital death.
     He drinks from flask then hands it to THIODULF
THIODULF *(raising flask)* To victory or the Val-hall!*
     He drinks from flask then hands it back to EYSTEIN

---

son of Jorn (Norse mythology) Thor, hammer-wielding god of storms and strength, etc.
Val-hall (Norse mythology) Valhalla, the majestic hall in Asgard ruled over by Odin, where he receives and feasts the souls of those fallen heroes selected by the Valkyries (for which see note on **Hildr**, pg 75)

Eystein Orre, what is't you dwell on with such
A darkling brow?
  Pause
EYSTEIN For how many wars have we rode the whale's way?
And how many Jut* towns've flared in our wake?
Fyen – Hedeby – Thioda – all burned for their
Defiance.
THIODULF And what fleet could Svein claim after
Nis!*
EYSTEIN Yet the Dane fight is not done.
Why now course the widths – for west women?
THIODULF For ring gold – and west women!
EYSTEIN   Ah, well then!
THIODULF For glory, War Chief – to fortify renown.
  Pause
EYSTEIN Bestow thyself, Thiodulf – the king's approaching.
  Exit THIODULF
Must chance be mooted,* Eystein? What hast
Thou else? A hut but no home – thy wife
In Nifelheim.* *(Pause)* But leave this ballast i' the shoals.
Thy ship is o'erladen.*
  *Enter HARDRADA with LEIF and other Norsemen. FRIREK
  enters separately.*
HARDRADA Frirek – art thou war-ready?
FRIREK   I throb for 't.
HARDRADA What beasts are those th't burnish thy vessel?
FRIREK Thou knowest well: the wolf and bear – blood-eyed,
With teeth and claws – tongues for the throat gush.

Jut Danish; of Denmark – from "Jutland," geographical term for the peninsula 'jutting' out into the North Sea which comprises mainland Denmark
what fleet…Nis most of King Svein of Denmark's navy was either destroyed or seized by Hardrada's forces during ship-to-ship fighting in the Battle of Nis River c. 1062
mooted made moot
Nifelheim (Norse mythology) underworld realm of mists and ice
leave this…o'erladen when a longship or knarr was heavily freighted ballast stones were often cast overboard to reduce draft and/or enhance stability – this was done while a ship was still near shore because the water was calmer there and the stones could later be retrieved for reuse

LEIF   Heed the war horn, Frirek.
HARDRADA   Lendermen,* make aboard.
   Exeunt all but HARDRADA and EYSTEIN
                                           Worthy Eystein,
Where is the West Lord?
EYSTEIN   At the harbor's head,
Folk King, awaiting our passage.
HARDRADA   Still dost
Thou doubt of him?
EYSTEIN   His sword oath will be kept.
HARDRADA   This heart-sure rede* pleases me to hear.
Go – get thee aboard – fasten our battle flag
For the signal time.
   Exit EYSTEIN. He kneels.
Warlike Wode – and Jesu, whose throne sits high
Over Hlidskjalf: lords of the nine worlds,
Rise up from thy slain-seats to still the salt ways,*
And speed us with summoning breath to thy bounty.
   He prays silently, then rises
Beserkmen: Tyr* invites. Make loose
Thy mooring lines. Now, noble Orre:
Raise Land Ravager.* *(Offstage acclamation. Exiting.)* Hoist
   our slaughter sign!
   Louder acclamation. Exit.

Lendermen   akin to "Hearthmen" (see note on pg 74) and meaning "men worthy of honor" in Old Norse
rede   (archaic) counsel; advice
Warlike Wode…salt ways   Hardrada, though nominally a Christian, invokes Odin and Jesus together, blending the two religious traditions; "Hlidskjalf" is the magic throne in Odin's palace of Valaskjalf ("seat of the slain") from which he can survey all nine regions of the universe; "salt ways" is a kenning for ocean
Tyr   (Norse mythology) god of war
Land Ravager   the king's standard, a triangular flag featuring a raven in flight

Act III scene 1: England. Chichester, near the southern coast.

Enter HAROLD at one side and two LORDS opposite. He greets them.

HAROLD Thou'st served past thy term already, friend.
LORD 1 Still, your highness, we feel inconstant thus departing.
HAROLD Do not – only suffer your wives' reproofs for
  So long a tenure here. There's neither wind
  Nor summer left with which the duke may sail.
  Get thee home.
    Exeunt LORD 1 & 2
  Bosham – mine's the kingdom now – and where'er
  God'll wake me.
    Enter LORD 3 & 4
LORD 3 Goodbye – and health attend your majesty.
LORD 4 Speed you well, sire.
HAROLD   Thank you, sirs –
  The same unto you both.
    Exeunt LORD 3 & 4
  But – be it not in Wessex for some while.
    Enter THEGN
THEGN Your majesty, I have thy last instruction?
HAROLD Yes, my friend – but a few more weeks. Some
  Force must be kept in arms there and, joined
  Together, the earls' detachments* make a potent
  Warranty.
THEGN   Then I'll to York. God bless
  Your majesty.
HAROLD   Thanks for your humble service,
  Thegn – convey the like to Edwin and
  His brother.
    Exit THEGN. Enter STIGAND.

---

joined together...detachments Harold refers to each earl's contingent of housecarls, since he has evidently dismissed both the northern and southern fyrd

Archbishop Stigand, the Nativity* is past –
What makes your grace in Chichester –
Are thy dues arreared?
STIGAND   Oh, my astounding
Liege, incontestable sovereign –
The devil take that dirty duke – 'tis well
I found thee here – Wight is a vile voyage.
HAROLD   I did not know you'd visited.
STIGAND   Oh no – but I had meant to, most holily.
Now to speak of the tithes, royal highness,
Collected from the parish here, I dare say
They are lucrative, but Chichester –
Which seems a dossal* unruly – lies not
Within the confines of my diocese –
Neither, though very nearly* –
And his sacristan* informs me that the bishop
Is quite breathing, though still in some discomfort
From a chicken bone he did choke upon
At Whitsun.* Indeed, I've had several missives since,
All most solicitously detailed,
Purporting to his full recovery therefrom,
And indicating, moreover, that the bone
Is now an object of some marvel to
The populace.
HAROLD   I must see this bone.
Archbishop, hast thou not come with news
Of some less fortunate prelate?*

Nativity Christian feast day commemorating the birth of Mary, celebrated in early September
seems a dossal i.e. somewhat or a little bit; a dossal is an ornamental cloth hung behind an altar or at the sides of a chancel
lies not within...very nearly the ecclesiastical holdings under Stigand's control at this time – and from which he drew considerable incomes – included the archbishopric of Canterbury and the wealthy see of Winchester, each of which embraced a large number of estates in southern England
sacristan clergy member charged with taking care of a church and its contents
Whitsun aka Pentecost, Christian holiday commemorating the descent of the Holy Spirit upon Christ's disciples (Acts 2:1-31), celebrated on the seventh Sunday after Easter
prelate cleric of high rank such as a bishop, abbot, or cardinal

STIGAND   You are too shrewd,
  Your highness. Romsey, sire – the abbot there
  Is dead. Oh, it is painful, sire, as he was
  A dear fellow of my youth – or shared
  His name – I never learned the truth.
HAROLD   No?
  And what name was that?
STIGAND   Stephen, sire –
  It was less common then.
HAROLD   Archbishop, hast thou
  No shame?
STIGAND   It is true, great king, I lack
  That article. The flesh sealed me too
  Acquisitive – but the Lord hath raised me up
  And hallowed my cupidity.
HAROLD   Well,
  Godliness with contentment is great gain.*
  Knowest thou Sheppey priory?*
STIGAND   Oh yes.
HAROLD Of what hath happened there?
STIGAND   The prioress –
  Stabbed by her kitchener – most wretched man.
  I, myself, was once near mauled by him for
  Complaining of his broth, though it was
  Not hearty. Alack. But Sheppey is a fen.
  Romsey –
HAROLD   An island fen, your excellency,
  With naught but sea air to recommend it,
  And the odd nun. As I recall, its revenue
  Is sparse, and the swamps there teem with fugitives.
  Thou art reputed for thy sternness.
STIGAND   Am I?
HAROLD And sternness is what's needed there – the cook

Godliness…great gain 1 Timothy 6:6
priory small monastery or convent governed by a prior or prioress

Has been executed, but several of
His culinary cohorts still roam
The bogs. Whereas they are lapsed pagans
And practice their unspeakable rites in full view
Of the ghasted sisters, they must be coaxed
Forthwith to reconversion – or the next
Prioress – whosoever holds the benefice* –
May likewise perish, and for broth that's scarcely thicker.
(Aside) Perhaps I jest too much in this. *(Aloud)* Archbishop –

STIGAND   Pagans, you say? Before the sisters? *(Aside)* Nineteen, I think – though one lacked arms – eighteen and a half then – and how many hectares – no, no, not all bog – bring in more oxen – yes – the sheep, though –

HAROLD   Archbishop, I should tell thee –

STIGAND   Exalted majesty, I am decided. Abbot Scolland of Saint Athelwines – a most sapient man – and unusually robust – lately remarked to me, though only after my discreetest urging, that he knew not why he'd been endowed with a certain office but that he loved the Lord, besides which,
Only a damn fool had demurred at it.
Well, I too love the Lord, oh regal one,
And all His beloved creatures – not least
Those who most profit salvation –
Nor am I fool enough to balk at this
Great benefice – therefore, I most
Sagaciously accept.

HAROLD   Really, Archbishop –

STIGAND   No more shall these loathsome heathens
Flourish their carnal implements before
Our wholesome nuns. No more shall
They worship such outmoded gods, nor
Invoke them to do mischief on priests they do
Not like. And no more shall they threaten men

---

benefice ecclesiastical office or post that guarantees the holder a fixed amount of property and/or income

    With tenderizing – or murder them – ever
    Again – for gastronomical critique.
HAROLD   What a daunting proselytic task this seems –
    Are you certain of your resolve, Archbishop?
STIGAND   No, I am not, munificent liege, but I am
    Of the Everlasting, whose love has fortified
    My folly.
    Enter SEA CAPTAIN
HAROLD   Your excellency, I am humbled
    By the honest greed and rich complacence
    Of thy faith – I have never met thy like
    For either. May both, like leathern reins,
    Callus thine unproven hands, and keep
    Thee couraged toward the fight. For off
    Must thou go – or rather on – onward,
    To Sheppey!
STIGAND   Bounteous lord, but one word more.
    Regarding Romsey –
HAROLD   There is no time for that –
    Go – go, Archbishop – think of the suffering nuns!
STIGAND   Yes, but –
HAROLD   And yields!
STIGAND   Ah – well –
    Exit STIGAND
HAROLD   Clavering!
SEA CAPTAIN   No, sire, he left to join his fyrdsmen –
    Though they're surely gone by now.
HAROLD   Oh yes, of course – thou hast his aspect.
SEA CAPTAIN   From Denmark, your majesty.
    He gives HAROLD a letter
HAROLD *(scanning letter)* Denmark – well, that's nearly
    Flemish.*
    But this is stale intelligence, reported

Denmark...nearly Flemish Harold hoped to learn that Tostig was settled in Flanders, where he'd earlier urged his brother to seek refuge

>   Weeks ago. Surely he's put off
>   By now – *(Aside)* or else the tides abate.
> SEA CAPTAIN   Sire, thy ships are all that's not disbanded.
> HAROLD   I will ride to London, Captain – you may
>   See them 'round. Safe journey.
>   *Exit SEA CAPTAIN*
>   The requiem hath ended, brother – the torches
>   Have burned down. How long wilt thou heap
>   This rankness on thyself? Thou art too keen
>   For 't. Is there not some other way?
>   Strand thyself, Tostig – don't wreck thee in
>   This selfish storm.
>   *Exit*

Act III scene 2: England. Northumbria, near Scarborough.

Several Norsemen cross the smoky stage, laughing perhaps, and dragging bodies, booty, or both. Then enter TOSTIG and a messenger.

TOSTIG *(to messenger)* Take this then, just as I say 't. *(Dictating)* I'm returned with Norway, who intends upon the kingdom. Scarborough burns. We make for York. I've forced more than I had occasion. Or it has forced – something – doesn't matter – the posies grow without us – whole unblushing banks of 'em. *(Pause)* These Norsemen, they are sturdy brutes – Harold better be in trim. *(Pause)* Edith, was he not – but let that go. *(To messenger)* Here! *(Takes letter and writes something, then seals and hands it back to messenger)* London and back if thou'd have all – here's a moiety.* *(Gives messenger money)* Sirrah! – Bring me her reply. *(Exit messenger)* I should've writ despisingly – or not at all. *(Pause)* To hell with it – I only fit the rigging.

---

moiety   portion; half

Enter HARDRADA accompanied by other Norsemen
HARDRADA   Where gallops that Englishman?
TOSTIG   To those friends I told of.
HARDRADA   Good. Come, West Lord, you must lead us
   Up the river ways. Our bright ships
   Will cleave this reeking smoke.
TOSTIG   Then thou hast slain enough?
HARDRADA   Many here are dead – soul-departed –
   But life threads end – even the Christ god
   Dies in the weave. Now come – away.
   We'll be more feared for this.
   Exeunt

Act III scene 3: Normandy. The mouth of the Dives. A field tent.

WILLIAM is dozing. FITZ-OSBERN's entrance awakens him.

WILLIAM   Well?
FITZ-OSBERN   I' the north, sire, still i' the north.*
WILLIAM   And? There is more.
FITZ-OSBERN   The harvest here's
   Foredone.
WILLIAM   Say on.
FITZ-OSBERN   My lord –
WILLIAM   Say on, man!
FITZ-OSBERN   The forests and the village pens are empty,
   Sire. How do you propose we should be fed?
WILLIAM   Rationally, of course, or wouldst thou starve thy
   reason
   With this puling? What more?!
FITZ-OSBERN   If
   The wind does not turn, sire –

---

still i'the north   the wind continues to blow in a southerly direction, making a channel crossing all but impossible for William's fleet

WILLIAM   It will turn.
FITZ-OSBERN   Yes, certainly, but it may not – and if
    You don't release these men before the frosts
    Then you pervert your cause – it seems unreasoned –
    And the charm of it'll deliquesce ere spring.
WILLIAM   Think you so – that I should turn them out?!
FITZ-OSBERN   My lord, a few – of scanter note – already
    Have decamped. And there've been heard, of late,
    Some scattered murmurs of defeasance.
WILLIAM   What is't they say?
FITZ-OSBERN   That the season's passed – that you ignore
    Or spite the perils. And these, together with
    The general want of food, conspire them,
    By slow degrees, toward dereliction.
WILLIAM   And yet withal, you think that they'll return
    In spring?
FITZ-OSBERN   My lord, I do – if let go now.
WILLIAM   And if they don't, what then?! What wouldst thou –
    Crouch into a pillory for whores to mock at?!
    Oh, there'd be no end – you should be laughed at
    To the grave – thy name gouged off thy tomb.
        Pause
    Cast off an army? Still a bobbing fleet?!
    I will enforce my claim – my right!
FITZ-OSBERN   Perhaps.
    The barons will soon enforce some action.
WILLIAM   Let them try!
        Pause. FITZ-OSBERN starts to leave.
                            Fitz-Osbern!
        FITZ-OSBERN turns
                            We'll sail, tomorrow –
    East – up to the Somme. 'Twill halve the crossing…
    And ease our want.
FITZ-OSBERN   Yes, my lord.

WILLIAM   You may
  Inform the men.
    FITZ-OSBERN starts to leave again
                 The wind will turn, Fitz-Osbern.
FITZ-OSBERN   Yes – so you've said.
    Exit FITZ-OSBERN

Act III scene 4: England. Northumbria. A hall in York.

EDWIN and MORCAR sit at one side of a large table provided with numerous chairs.

MORCAR   This is past all reason.
EDWIN   And when you've had your filthy sport with her,
  What then, wilt into thy soiling?!
MORCAR   Brother –
EDWIN *(ignoring him)* Better plucked out by the root.
MORCAR   Edwin, you must forbear – she is the daughter
  Of the ealdorman.
EDWIN   Aye, she's the ealdorman's –
  And so's his stable boy! I've heard it spoke
  Enough – a fool could note the likeness.
MORCAR   I won't believe it.
EDWIN   Truth is rife with blemishment.
MORCAR   Have you even ridden –
EDWIN   On my lone, aborted
  'Tempt, I quit the place appalled, when through
  A stinking barn I spied them – all together –
  Cavorting on the paddock!
MORCAR   Which meaneth what –
  That she is not disdainful? That she craves
  Her father's company? And you would twist
  These into – something wrong – unnatural.

Enter THEGN and several LORDS followed by AELDRED and EALDORMAN. EDWIN and MORCAR then rise. All seat themselves after AELDRED.

EDWIN   I but report them as they are. Archbishop.
Ealdorman. *(Aside to MORCAR)* You must choose whom you'll regard.

MORCAR   Good morning, your excellency. Sir.

AELDRED   Good morning – and blessed be all. Morcar – Mercia –
Ealdorman. *(Pause)* Please – proceed unstintingly –
I'm here ex mero motu* – to be informed,
Not interfere. Earl – please.

MORCAR *(rising)*   Well – uh –
Little has changed since yesternight – his fleet
Was banked at Spurn Head – we think they're in
The Humber now, some three hundred or so,
Of painted longships mostly.

LORD   What about the king's brother, sire?

ANOTHER LORD   Yeah, is he with 'em?

ANOTHER LORD   This is all Tostig's doing!

MORCAR   I'm not certain –

THEGN   Several ships in the front are almost certainly his, sire, and he was recognized at Scarborough.
   Enter a messenger, who whispers briefly to THEGN then exits. THEGN in turn whispers to EDWIN.

LORD   Then I'm satisfied.

ANOTHER LORD   This time he dies.

ANOTHER LORD   The devil be expecting him.

EDWIN   Good! He's landed at Riccall.

AELDRED   By the saints, that's not ten miles from here!

THEGN   We must advance.
   Affirmative exclamations from lords

LORD   Let's march.

ANOTHER LORD   Hack 'em hence!

ex mero motu (Latin) "of my own accord"

EALDORMAN I say –
ANOTHER LORD We'll murder the slaves!
EALDORMAN I say –
LORD Hush – quiet there – let's hear the ealdorman.
EALDORMAN Perhaps we should more cautiously prepare
   Ourselves – the fyrdsmen are only just
   Returning. Why not make a brief withdrawal –
   For a few days merely – until more men
   Arrive?
LORD   What you say is cowardice!
MORCAR The ealdorman is no coward, sir.
THEGN   Honored
   Lord, your action would invite a siege.
LORD They'd raze the city – Tostig'd flesh* them to it.
MORCAR *(to EALDORMAN)* If we march now we can seize the
   most
   Advantaged ground.
EALDORMAN *(to MORCAR)* Yes, but will you have
   The men to keep it?
EDWIN *(overhearing)*   More will not be needed:
   Godwinson is a rash and stupid fellow – he
   And his brutish pack of raiders can no more
   Form a battle line than 's many Scots –
   Or mongrels – their spear-sense died with Canute.
EALDORMAN *(ignoring EDWIN)* Morcar, these men are savages,
    'tis true,
   But capably devised – fearsome. If you wait –
EDWIN   – Morcar, what shall be the course
   That this day takes – speak out and so end
   Contention. *(Aside to MORCAR)* Thou knowest well our means –
   The scope and breadth of actions we might safely
   Undertake – so choose.

---

flesh (falconry) encourage a raptor to hunt by feeding it flesh from a kill

Act III scene 5: England. Northumbria. South of York, near Fulford Gate.

Enter EYSTEIN, TOSTIG, GUNNAR, THIODULF, and other Norsemen

EYSTEIN   Then hast thou, Westman, no brace in thy breast –
   No blooming clutch for a lass?
TOSTIG   I live too wildly
   For such reposing, Orre – nor 've I the need of 't.
EYSTEIN   What hast thou need of then?
TOSTIG   Not flowers, man.
   Norseman, why do you persist with me?
   Because you are less heathenish than these
   Do you think we shall be friendly?
EYSTEIN   This is sour word-spite, even for
   An English.
TOSTIG   Think'st thou? I have a woman – or –
   There's one I do not fully understand.
EYSTEIN   Just one? And she too is English?
TOSTIG   She is, and of the world about.
EYSTEIN   Ah –
   Mine was all of home.
TOSTIG   Home. Was she?
   But what a place is that? An thou didst love her
   Whatever mattered where? I'll none of home.
   She was – where'er she was – I'll none of home.
   'Tis the notion a child clings to, as it would
   Its mother's skirts before she shoos him out
   Of doors. A man does not roof himself illusions,
   He pulls them down.
EYSTEIN   Illusions?
TOSTIG   Lies – fancy.
EYSTEIN   And thou wouldst foot through such a wilderness?

Thou art more bold than Eystein. But –
A distant rumbling sound
                                                Earth stirs.
Thiodulf – fare ahead along the road edge
And see what com'st.
THIODULF hesitates
GUNNAR *(to THIODULF)* Lackest thou pluck without
Thy instrument?
EYSTEIN   Gunnar – 'twere better both you go.
Exeunt GUNNAR and THIODULF. The sound grows louder.
(To TOSTIG) Some folk-friends of thine?
TOSTIG   I think not.
GUNNAR *(offstage)* Steeds approach!
EYSTEIN Unsling axes – shoulder shields. *(Pause)* Stand ready.
THIODULF *(offstage)* 'Tis Leif! 'Tis Leif Andreasson!
EYSTEIN He's hardly left.
LEIF *(offstage)* Where is Eystein Orre?!
Enter LEIF, ARNULF, GUNNAR, and THIODULF
EYSTEIN Leif Andreasson – what prompts such swift returning?
LEIF The English – they have come out to meet us.
EYSTEIN Strangely fate-eager. But tell us, Leif,
How rates this English army?
LEIF Weak – with too much shine for spear-strength.
This is proof untested* – unmettled – meet for
A Northman's onslaught.
EYSTEIN   And what of their array?
LEIF Locked close at the lind' wall,* but sprawling –
O'erstretched – thinned through the sinew.
ARNULF Noble Orre, they lie but half a league distant.
EYSTEIN Half a league?
GUNNAR Where is Hardrada?!

proof untested armor that has not been tested (as was customary) to ensure its effectiveness
lind' wall armies of the period typically fought in shoulder to shoulder formation holding their shields before them to establish a defensive wall; these shields were often fashioned from linden wood because it was easily carved

ARNULF *(ignoring GUNNAR)* Aye.
EYSTEIN   Gunnar Streelkin:
    Lead our bonde troops* up to the foe-facing.
    Arnulf Ulson: with thy stoutest hearth friends
    Stay the bearsarks – till the king strides forth
    They must not reach the field. West Lord: best look
    To thy men. *(Aside)* Thrill to the bidding,* Eystein –
    Let the fight be all. *(To LEIF)* Quickly, now – to the war king.
LEIF   Aye – we'll greet him as Frek and Ger!*
    Exeunt all but TOSTIG
TOSTIG   Let them – bring all – clog up the ground –
    So I stand wasted by.
      Pause
    For what is't demanded? Nothing says "that"
    I should do – or "forswear" the other. Nothing says
    Keep t'the order but concupiscent priests
    And their empty sooth* of words.
    "Seize – here – this o'er all the others" –
    There's no such augury, just tongues with sick'ning reasons.
    Say out: "What should I do?" – That I cannot.
    Then what concern is it of thine? Play the pawn –
    Perchance survive – there be no other reason.
      Exit

Act III scene 6: England. Northumbria. Fulford Gate.

Enter EDWIN, MORCAR, and THEGN followed by soldiers

EDWIN   Such a noise of hollering – like raucous children.
THEGN   But with swords instead of sticks.

---

bonde troops Norse levy generally consisting of farmers, merchants, and craftsmen
bidding invitation or summons to battle
Frek and Ger (Norse mythology) two giant wolves that attend on Odin. Pronounce with vowels short and the "g" hard.
sooth [1] truth; reality [2] (obsolete) blandishment; enticement

EDWIN   Send
  The whole line forward – every thegn
  And cottar.*
THEGN   With no reserve?
EDWIN   Engage them all –
  These armed thugs do not merit tactics.
      Exit THEGN with soldiers
MORCAR *(looking off)* Edwin, who are those just joined the field?
EDWIN Upon what side?! Keep thy head, brother.
MORCAR Prowling there along the rise, cloaked in skins –
  Some are wearing claws and the heads of wolves.
EDWIN Ignore them – they are bugbears meant to stir
  Thy fear. Viking sots. *(Aside)* And Godwinson –
  Soon shalt thou be foulness – thy brisk taunts
  Congealed in putrefaction.
      Pause. He starts to leave.
  First the one, then –
MORCAR *(at the same time)* These are a different sort of men.
EDWIN   Morcar!
      Exit EDWIN, then MORCAR following

Act III scene 7: The same. Battle.

Battle sounds. Norsemen retreat over the stage and exit. Enter THEGN and a CAPTAIN leading English soldiers in pursuit.

CAPTAIN Keep on! Keep on! Drive them down the hill!
  Never'd I conceived the Norse such cowards!
THEGN They flee like men bred for it!
CAPTAIN   Keep on!
      Exeunt

---

cottar peasant farmer

Act III scene 8: The same. Battle continues.

Enter HARDRADA, LEIF, and other Norsemen retreating over the stage, one of them bearing the king's standard

LEIF   Unheeding host – their line-strength is gone!
HARDRADA   Hearthmen: glory nears – and weapons hunger –
   Halt thy retreats! Let sound the horn!
   Not a foot-length further shalt thou yield but turn…
   Steel to the fray, and shirk this battle ruse!
   Warhorn blown. The Norsemen charge back across the stage and meet the English as they enter. Fighting.
   Sound the second blast!
   Warhorn blown again. FRIREK and other berserkers enter and join. The English are beaten back. Exeunt, fighting.

Act III scene 9: The same. Battle continues.

Battle sounds. Enter MORCAR, CAPTAIN, and others in the English army.

MORCAR   We are beaten – the ealdorman's horribly killed!
   Where is Edwin?!
CAPTAIN   He hath fled, my lord.
MORCAR   Fled – that cannot be.
CAPTAIN   Then I mistook him,
   Sire.
MORCAR   Didst thou?! I must find him.
   Exit MORCAR. Enter English and Norsemen fighting, the English in retreat. Among the Norsemen are EYSTEIN, LEIF, GUNNAR, and FRIREK.
CAPTAIN   Steady, men! Steady! Hold together there!

> *CAPTAIN is killed. The English retreat pell-mell. All of the Norsemen except the berserkers halt their pursuit. Enter HARDRADA followed by THIODULF.*

HARDRADA   Berserkmen, abate thy furies – lay by!
   Allfod* is gleeful – glad is the grim one.
FRIREK   We rage for more!
HARDRADA *(ignoring FRIREK)* The White Christ* too beams in
   our triumph –
   For his wounds shall we spare the craven –
   Let cowards flee.
   > *FRIREK growls*
   Frirek, thou shalt ha' thy surfeit:
   Treasure hordes, deep-piled from the burg,
   Bowing the feast boards – and ripest hearth maids,
   Plumped with the plenty – and ales, and mead. Enough!
   Honored Orre.
   > *EYSTEIN comes forward*
   Chief Lender, return
   To the drakkar with our army's bulk
   And make ready the fame-feast –
   (Aside to EYSTEIN) Thou shalt ha' thy pick among the dames.
   (Aloud) I'll with the West Lord into Yorkish-town
   For gold-taking and to set forth further dues.
EYSTEIN *(motioning to THIODULF)* War King.
HARDRADA   Skald,* send up the song!
THIODULF   Then so it goes:
   Wave gatherings clogged the whale paths –
   Aegir* threatened – and the Northmen hard travailed.
   Fey fog shrouded the foe shores –

Allfod (Norse mythology) meaning "Allfather" in Old Norse, this is one of Odin's many names
White Christ name given Jesus by the Vikings, probably due to the white robes worn by all newly baptized Christian converts
skald Scandinavian poet skilled esp. in the composition and recitation of poems glorifying heroes and their deeds
Aegir (Norse mythology) god of the sea

Nornish* hull-bane – many brave ones were lost –
And the Northmen hard travailed.
Far from kinfolk have we come –
Weathered much – hard wert our travails –
But in the storm of spears the Northmen have prevailed!
  Acclamation
EYSTEIN Well turned, Thiodulf.
THIODULF Still – it seemeth short a verse. *(Exiting)* Suppose, Peradventure,* instead of ending at...
  Exeunt HARDRADA and others at one side, EYSTEIN, THIO-DULF, FRIREK, etc. opposite

Act III scene 10: The coast of Ponthieu. A rampart above St-Valery-sur-Somme.

  FITZ-OSBERN in conversation with two BARONS

BARON 1 That's all well and good but I've a man stabbed.
BARON 2 And I've a woman raving in my camp.
FITZ-OSBERN And how is it singing brought all this about?
BARON 1 Well – some did pay her.
FITZ-OSBERN To more than sing?
BARON 1 That is my understanding.
BARON 2 She danced too as I believe – I'm told delightfully.
FITZ-OSBERN So it would seem. Will the fellow survive?
BARON 1 I expect so.
FITZ-OSBERN And hath he means?
BARON 1 Very little, sir.
FITZ-OSBERN Then you shall stead the father.

Nornish (Norse mythology) of or pertaining to the Norns – comparable to the Fates of Greek mythology, the Norns spin the life threads of human beings and determine each ones extent
peradventure possibly; perhaps

Enter MESSENGER

MESSENGER The duke commands you to your vessels.

Exit MESSENGER

BARON 2 *(looking off)* The lantern's lit on the Mora!*

FITZ-OSBERN Yes, I can see that. Return to your men. There'll be no time for further action – mend the matter.

BARONS start to leave. FITZ-OSBERN gathers some articles.

BARON 2 You heard him – come and claim the girl.

BARON 1 Just send her over.

BARON 2 But I have – she keeps coming back. Her wits are gone.

Exeunt BARONS

FITZ-OSBERN *(looking off)* Quelle chance!*

Enter WILLIAM

WILLIAM Art through with thy dispute?

FITZ-OSBERN *(somewhat startled)*   I am – just.

WILLIAM It's held since daybreak now – I'll wait no longer. And you had thought it foolish to remain.

FITZ-OSBERN Imprudent, my lord.

WILLIAM   And what think you now?

FITZ-OSBERN That this is a most fortunate turn –

WILLIAM   Here it comes.

FITZ-OSBERN If sway be held o'er our assemblage.

WILLIAM My god, man – hang thy caveats – Thou art worse than that infernal monk!

FITZ-OSBERN *(ignoring him)* An open sea may quell them for a time.

WILLIAM And I will for the rest.

FITZ-OSBERN May you be not long engaged.

WILLIAM We leave at once!

He starts to leave then turns back

This is an historic even –*

Mora William's flagship – lighting the lantern on her mast indicated that the fleet was about to sail
Quelle chance! (French) "What luck!"
even (archaic) evening

From tomorrow will be dated epochs!
Exit WILLIAM. FITZ-OSBERN puts on his cloak and finishes gathering articles.
FITZ-OSBERN   I do so loathe the sea.
Exit

Act III scene 11: England. Northumbria. Camp of the Norsemen at Riccall.

Night. TOSTIG is slumped over, evidently drunk. Enter LEIF.

LEIF   West Lord?
TOSTIG   More canst 'ou want?!
LEIF   Godwinson?!
TOSTIG   What – is't tomorrow? *(Seeing LEIF)* The saturnalia's ended.
LEIF   At dawn we foot for Stamford Bridge.
TOSTIG   Then when it comes send to wake me.
LEIF   Be thou roused and ready.
   Exit LEIF
TOSTIG   What's that, soused and unsteady?! Ah, it matters not. I am ill-used – ill-used, I say…– like a goddamn whore – and seasick…with uh, all the, uh…boats…– no, not boats…
   He sleeps for a short time then EDITH enters, disguised as a Norseman
EDITH   *(waking him)* Tostig.
TOSTIG   What laddie, bad dreams? Thy helmet won't protect thee.
EDITH   *(removing disguise)* Tostig, look at me.
TOSTIG   Edith?! Yet – how came you here? I had sent couriers but –
EDITH   From Northumbria? – I received none at Bosham.
TOSTIG   Bosham?!

EDITH Harold sent me word.
TOSTIG You were not at court?
EDITH No.
TOSTIG And you've come alone?
EDITH Here, drink this.
    She gives him water
TOSTIG You should not be here, Edith.
EDITH   Nor should you.
TOSTIG Yes – well – there's no succor for that.
EDITH Leave with me now.
TOSTIG   Indeed.
EDITH   Leave with me now.
TOSTIG I've thought what else I could do, Edith –
    Thought on't till I exhausted all the store –
    But I'd nothing real to pledge against a quittance.
    Soon I will:
    Tomorrow morning – today – or do you know? –
    Our ransom meeting's set, wherewith entails*
    My propertied release from whorish bondage
    To take up what I will.
EDITH   And what will you?
TOSTIG A fine Yorkish manor, very near the mint.
EDITH Prithee,* then?
TOSTIG   I had enticed you away.
EDITH Indeed.
TOSTIG   And been less vexed awhile.
EDITH Yes – till it came back again.
    Pause
TOSTIG Why did you come here, Edith?
    Was it to reform me?
    Have you not given up on that?!
    An I even could inure me to this world

---

wherewith entails with which thing follows
prithee (archaic) contraction of "I pray thee," used in polite requests

>   Or find regret in anything I've done
>   I could not long live in it.
>   There's a tedium o' the earth I cannot bide,
>   A complacence in its wiles – seasons – tides –
>   That with such regular commotion'd sweep me under
>   Did not sometimes a wayward, unfletched notion
>   Nock, take hold, and fling me on.*

EDITH   But can you not perceive? It comes from you –
   You inflict upon this world malaise
   To trouble it with violence as 'twere no other aim,
   Or those all vain besides.
   Tostig, what is it you can't reconcile?
   What ancient anger or remorse? Say what it is.
   Have done with suffering. Let there be an end.

TOSTIG   There is no end – there is not ever ending
   But it wraps around again and spoils the heretofore.
   (Sotto voce) Forgiveness palls…and shudders at its weedy reach.

EDITH   At what, Tostig?! I know thy history.
   Come away with me – leave this place.

TOSTIG   I will leave, soon enough.

EDITH   We must go now.
   Pause

TOSTIG   Is it possible?!

EDITH   He doesn't know I'm here.

TOSTIG   How long?

EDITH   I think…he is not coming to Riccall.
   Pause

TOSTIG   I have no words but, for what I most feel,
   It is relief.

EDITH   He loves you Tostig.
   So do I.

TOSTIG   Then stay awhile here with me.

Did not…fling me on arrows that have not been feathered or "fletched" will be much less stable in flight; an arrow is fitted to the bowstring for shooting by means of a carved notch or groove called a "nock"

EDITH There is no time.
TOSTIG   Yet you think there'll be another?!
EDITH Stop.
TOSTIG What else shall I say?
   What proof or protestation else
   Remains to give thee?!
   I adore you, Edith – there it is –
   But as for leaving, do not ask that now.
EDITH Why did I ask before?!
   I knew you'd not be saved
   Even as I reached the stable –
   Yet here I am, foolishly,
   Having ridden all the miles,
   Stolen here to see you one more time.
   Alas, why is it not till now
   Does all my hope sublime?*
      She breaks down
   Oh Tostig, what's to be done?
TOSTIG The heat and journey have fatigued you.
EDITH No – no – it is despair unseats me –
   And shame – and incipient disgust.
TOSTIG If thou know'st another way –
EDITH Thou hast unfixed the rest – there is none!
   I cannot lose you both.
      Long pause
TOSTIG Such a close night portends a steamy day.
   Hast 'ou ever rounded hostages?
   Really, 'tis a tedious affair.
   So many oaths, so much tallying of names.
   And someone always, unaccountably, gets bludgeoned.
EDITH Tostig, please –
TOSTIG   With a hot day blooming
   And a long march ahead, I say:

sublime pass directly from a solid to a vapor state; vaporize

For such perfect drudgery as this – life is –
What recks it* shield or armor? Like as not
We'll leave our byrnies* at Riccall.
EDITH   That is not what I mean.
TOSTIG   It's how I choose to take it.
EDITH   Yes…I know.
> *Offstage voices, then several Norsemen enter and cross the stage. TOSTIG pulls EDITH toward him in an effort to conceal her. They kiss. Shortly after the Norsemen exit he starts to release her.*

Hold me for a time.
> *Pause. They remain close.*

TOSTIG   I don't repent me what I've done,
Only that it hurt those undeserving.
> *Pause*

You should go. Harold will look after ye –
You'll not want.
EDITH   And who will after you?
TOSTIG   Let it be the devil, that thou might'st come
And rescue me in Dis.*
EDITH *(embracing him)*   What makes you think
I'd come again – or that I could succeed?
TOSTIG   I shan't believe this the last I'll see of thee.
Still – for what there is in it: farewell.
> *Exit EDITH*

What recks it Of what importance is
byrnie protective chainmail shirt or tunic
Dis hell; the underworld

Act III scene 12: England. Northumbria. Stamford Bridge.

HARDRADA, TOSTIG, LEIF, GUNNAR, ARNULF, THIODULF, FRIREK, and other Norsemen, one of them holding the king's standard

LEIF   – the Serkland sieges –
  Those were towns tough for the taking.
GUNNAR   Arnulf Ulson was a nursling then.
ARNULF   But I have learned the ploys, and canst well recount
  The troubles had there.
THIODULF   Gunnar knows the scheme at Mosul – 'twas him
  That breached the floor when it fell about his head!
GUNNAR   Skald, thou wast not even in the passage.
LEIF   No, but Streelkin was, and so remained,
  Helm-dented, while his war band cleared the hall.
    Laughter
HARDRADA   Mosul – need-fires* rekindle at the mention –
  For then was Ulf among us, and with him Halldor,
  Best of sword friends.
LEIF   Bold warriors both.
    He observes something offstage
HARDRADA   Bitterly we parted.
ARNULF   Lo – dust clouds –
THIODULF   Thick as Sindri's smoke.*
ARNULF   They are coming down.
GUNNAR *(to THIODULF)* Too thick it is.
    Pause
FRIREK   Today slaughter-wolves feed!
LEIF *(to FRIREK)*   Thou senseth aright.
  (To HARDRADA) Ring Breaker, this is no hostage train –
  It is a fyrd army which confronts us,
  And with a mighty war chief at the head.

---

need-fire deep-seated longing; passionate need to achieve a desired end
Sindri's smoke (Norse mythology) that is, the smoke from Sindri's forge – Sindri was a dwarf and renowned blacksmith who worked tirelessly at his forge fashioning magical weapons (e.g. Thor's hammer) and other items for the gods

HARDRADA So may it be – aye – much deems it hostile.
　West Lord, thou hast surveyed the force
　And art most fit to descant on their bearing.
　Come forward – acquaint us with thy counsel.
TOSTIG It looks to be a hostile army, but,
　I suppose it could be some abject relations
　Mustering hither for pardon.
LEIF　　　　　　　　　　　Nonsense!
　This man hath no loyal kinfolk.
ARNULF Sure they'd not o'ertop the roadway.
HARDRADA *(looking off)* Eyes seize only edge-hate in those ranks.
TOSTIG Perhaps we should turn back – we are out-weaponed
　And undermanned…though we've beaten them already.
HARDRADA I've another counsel. Leif Andreasson:
　On three swift horses mount a trio of lads –
　Spur them with all speed to Eystein Orre.
　From the ship-beaks he will haste relief.
LEIF Aye, king.
　　Exit LEIF
TOSTIG You must order in this as seemeth fit.
　By no means is it my wish to retreat.
HARDRADA Then, with what war gear thou hast, prepare.
　Hearthmen: Orre may not come quick enough.
　If his fleetness fails – or in the spear-rush
　Wyrd warps our prowess – even so –
　Let it wend –
　The English'll get a hard go of it
　Afore we give us up for lost!

Act III scene 13: The same. Along the English lines.

Enter two SOLDIERS hailing amidst the army, part of which stands in formation onstage

SOLDIER 1   The king seeks a gentleman for the parley –
   Clavering! Call out where you are – I say –
   Lord Clavering!
SOLDIER 2   Clavering! Hie thee to the king's summons!
   Enter HAROLD
SOLDIER 1   Majesty, this man is unknown to us –
   Hath he some other title?
HAROLD   No other bestowals, sir, but he is here –
   On good word I have it. Lord Clavering,
   'Tis Harold now calls you out!
SOLDIER 2   We must go, my lord.
HAROLD *(ignoring SOLDIER 2)* Clavering!
SOLDIER 2   Pray, what is his name, sire? His family?
SOLDIER 1   Lord Clavering!
HAROLD   His name is – *(Somewhat louder)* it is Robert Fitz-Wimark.
ROBERT *(offstage)* I am Robert Fitz-Wimark.
SOLDIER 1   Your majesty, here is the gentleman you seek.
   Enter ROBERT
ROBERT *(surprised)* My liege!
HAROLD   Robert! Ah – 'tis well I've found ye –
   He shakes ROBERT's hand
   Though it be by but a dram, always
   Thy simple nearness evens out the humor.
ROBERT   Then 'tis well indeed. But truly, sire –
   On such a day as this –
   That you should seek for me! Why,
   It's twenty years since I've seen combat,
   Excepting boars – always excepting them –
   Besides which, I cut a poor soldier.

HAROLD   I won't believe it.
ROBERT   My own fyrdsmen must lead me in our drills.
HAROLD   Then perhaps it's best they're over.
SOLDIER 2   Your majesty.
HAROLD *(to SOLDIER 2)* A moment, sir – a moment.
  (To ROBERT) Robert, my intent is not to make thee general –
  Leastwise, not today. No –
  To speak true, it's for luck I sought thee out,
  And the hopeful influence o' thy nature:
  To carry terms with me to the parley.
ROBERT   Me, my lord? That is, of course! –
  If a sporting man may be of help.
  But sire, should you go?
HAROLD   I must – Tostig is with them. I'd thought perhaps,
  In thy company, he might prove more amenable.
ROBERT   My lord, Tostig never took to me,
  Nor t' none that I know save his majesty,
  Whose sufferance he oft keenly tested.
HAROLD   Yes – of course – 'twas a foolish notion.
  Well – attach thy men to my guard here –
  We'll ride out and see how he's disposed.
    Exeunt

Act III scene 14: The same. The Norse side.

HARDRADA, TOSTIG, LEIF, GUNNAR, ARNULF, THIODULF, FRIREK, and other Norsemen

ARNULF   A gang of English fast approaches.
    LEIF starts to leave with other Norsemen
HARDRADA   Keep by – let them ride the way –
  For what of ear-worth can they say?
  This doth gift time to our defense.

Pause

LEIF   Certes* by now they must see we'll not meet them.

Pause

GUNNAR   Either mad they are or daft.

TOSTIG   They are neither.

Enter HAROLD and ROBERT accompanied by English soldiers. HAROLD is wearing a bright surcoat.

HAROLD   Is Earl Tostig in this army?

TOSTIG *(coming forward)* You will find him here.

HAROLD   Your brother the king sends salutations
  And bids you: lay down your arms
  And take up Northumbria again.
  In return he asks only your fealty,
  And the pledge of a fair and merciful rule
  Over the people there.

TOSTIG   How very different
  This is from last winter's punity.*
  Had my brother the king but offered this then
  Perhaps the people had been better served,
  And fewer lives been lost. Or perhaps not –
  'Twould be moot to know.
  But say th't I accept this appeasing offer,
  What will you grant Hardrada for his troubles?

HAROLD   The king has also spoken of this,
  And he will give the Norseman
  Six feet of English ground, or somewhat more,
  As they say he is a taller man.

TOSTIG   It shan't e'er be said of a Godwinson
  That he once betrayed his nature. Go now,
  And tell King Harold to prepare for battle.

HAROLD   The king will bear grievously the news of your
  resolve,

---

certes   (archaic) certainly; surely. Pronounce as one syllable with a soft "s" to rhyme with "hurts."
punity   punitive treatment

And yet, withal, expect it as in keeping
With that courageous spirit you have always shown.
TOSTIG   I would not disappoint him in that.
HAROLD   Frater –
TOSTIG   Vale – ave atque vale.*
   Exeunt HAROLD, ROBERT, and English soldiers
HARDRADA   Who was that noble discoursed so well?
TOSTIG   The king.
HARDRADA   For far too long was this concealed!
No king on such a toss should 'scape
To tell the slaughter.
TOSTIG   It was a reckless act,
To be sure, and may be as you say,
But I saw what he had come to offer –
That I'd be his murderer if I betrayed him –
And I would rather die myself
Than in such wise strike him down.
HARDRADA   Damn! *(Pause)* Return to thy hearth band and forearm.
  (Looking off) He's a smaller fellow…but firm in his stirrups.
   Exit TOSTIG
LEIF   War King, the bondes* are but half-deployed.
   Pause
What wouldst thou?
HARDRADA   Hold for a spell.
GUNNAR *(to LEIF)* We cannot tarry here!
HARDRADA *(ignoring GUNNAR)* I shall compose upon this chance:
Sternly we'll strive 'gainst biting steel,
Courage-girt though byrnieless.

Frater…atque vale (Latin) "Brother, farewell – hail and farewell" – from the final line of an elegy written in tribute to his brother by the Roman poet Catullus. Harold's intent is to speak a few parting words in Latin to Tostig, thinking it unlikely any Norsemen nearby would understand the language. Tostig cuts him off. Approximate pronunciation: "FRAH-tair –" "WAH-lai – ah-WAHT-kwai WAH-lai."

bondes Norse levy (see note on pg 102). Pronounce as two syllables here with the "e" long.

Helmets shine – I have not mine –
It lies in a heap of armor.
GUNNAR *(to LEIF)* The battle-hedge will not be ready!
LEIF *(to GUNNAR)* Then thither, Streelkin – see that it is!
  Exit GUNNAR reluctantly
HARDRADA   These verses are poorly wrought – I must make better:
Skuld* hath bared us to the brunt:
Helms we have not – no, nor mail –
Nor bucklers* to bear with arms.
But we shall wield* us while we can,
And if our doom it be to die here,
Then we'll not begrudge our endings.
  Pause. He exchanges glances with FRIREK.
Arnulf Ulson, take Land Ravager
Up the ridge and plant it in our midst.
  Exeunt ARNULF, THIODULF, and others with standard
LEIF   Folk King, leave me a few brave warriors
And go – we'll hold the bridge long enough.
FRIREK   No!
  He steps onto the bridge, places his weapons before him, and begins to remove his garments
HARDRADA *(to LEIF)* Frirek alone will slay more English.
LEIF   But he is our fiercest.
HARDRADA   And thou the most cunning.
  (To FRIREK) Berserkman: don thy wolf-coat.
FRIREK   I'll leave it off.
  Sound of approaching troops
HARDRADA   What of thy fellow Wodesmen?* *(Pause)* Frirek?!
FRIREK   Go now!

Skuld (Norse mythology) meaning roughly "what ought to happen" in Old Norse, she is the Norn (see note on pg 106) most often associated with future events
buckler small round shield
wield (archaic) govern; manage
Wodesmen i.e. berserkers, who worshipped Odin in his capacity as god of warriors

HARDRADA So long then.
LEIF *(exiting, to FRIREK)* The Val-maids* will come for ye!
  Exeunt HARDRADA and LEIF
FRIREK Not as Gytha did.
  Sound of troops grows louder. FRIREK finishes stripping down, regirds, then kneels on one leg, waiting. When the English army enters, he bellows and attacks.

Act III scene 15: England. A beach on the southern coast near Pevensey.

Enter WILLIAM to the sound of waves crashing, followed at some distance by FITZ-OSBERN, ODO, and several BARONS. WILLIAM kneels to gather sand then rises, as an army meanwhile converges around him.

WILLIAM This earth that I here take up in my hands,
  It too now is Norman – mine to command –
  Mine and therefore yours if I should grant it,
  Each man fit to his deserving. So?
  What sayest to thy future sovereign?
FITZ-OSBERN We but wait upon your word.
WILLIAM *(looking at FITZ-OSBERN, then at BARONS)* Do you?!
BARON 1 Aye, my lord.
BARON 2 Aye.
BARON 3 Just give us leave.
  Pause
WILLIAM Ashore then if you'd earn of my largesse,
  And with me rid this kingdom of the regnant
  Perjurer!

Val-maids Valkyries; they were sometimes known as the "handmaidens" of Odin or Valhalla

SOLDIERS IN THE ARMY   Down with the apostate! Death to Godwinson!

Exeunt WILLIAM, FITZ-OSBERN, ODO, etc. to acclamation followed by army with drum and standards

FINIS.

Sources & Acknowledgements

This play draws largely on original and often contemporary source material, including but not limited to the Vita Aedwardi Regis, Gesta Normannorum Ducum, Bayeux Tapestry, Heimskringla, and Anglo-Saxon Chronicle.

The author would like to acknowledge a special debt owed the late David Howarth. It was his charming book, <u>1066: The Year of the Conquest</u>, that for good or for ill inspired this one.

Made in the USA
Columbia, SC
30 June 2025